SKIPPING THE LEARNING CURVE

SKIPPING THE LEARNING CURVE

Advanced Litigation Concepts and Strategies for New Lawyers

AARON SHECHET, ESQ.

Copyright © 2021 Aaron Shechet

All rights reserved. This book may not be reproduced, in whole or in part, without written permission from the publisher, except by a reviewer who may quote brief passages in a review; nor may any part of this book be reproduced, stored in a retrieval system, or transmitted in any form or by any means, electronic, mechanical, recording or other, without written permission from the publisher.

LawyeredUp Publishing
312 South Beverly Dr. #7244
Beverly Hills, CA 90212
Aaron@Shechet.com

Paperback ISBN: **978-1-7377319-0-0**
Kindle ISBN: **978-1-7377319-1-7**

CONTENTS

INTRODUCTION
The Secret to Litigation.......................... 1

PART I
Attitude Adjustment............................. 9

PART II
Beyond Basic Skills.............................. 31

PART III
Settlement Leverage Points and the
Keystone of the Case............................ 95

PART IV
Strategies and Counterstrategies................ 127

FINAL THOUGHTS
Finding Balance................................... 171

PREFACE

This book developed organically. Against the advice of almost everyone, my wife and I started our law firm right out of law school. There were plenty of books that new lawyers could read to answer common questions. If we needed to know procedure or a summary of the most important laws in a specific practice area, there were practice guides. If we needed to learn how to take a deposition or lead a trial, there were books on the subjects. We found books on managing a law office, books on organizing case files, and books on legal ethics.

But there were no books on litigation strategy.

Although we could easily find the options available in response to a complaint, there was nothing explaining how to choose one option over another. There was nothing explaining what a successful outcome to a lawsuit looks like. There was nothing explaining how to handle opposing counsel.

We were left teaching ourselves what a successful outcome in litigation looks like and how to get there. We did this by analyzing opposing counsel's work product and asking "is this good? What could they have done better? What could they have done that would have made us nervous about our case?" We analyzed our own results by spending countless hours asking "why did we win or lose this motion? What did we accomplish? Did this get our client closer to a successful outcome? What could we have done differently?" We kept track of our analysis from the start and reviewed those lessons along the way. This book puts those lessons into a usable form and, like a music "method," a logical progression.

Imagine being a young lawyer in Los Angeles in '70's. You have breakfast with other young lawyers at the local diner before work. You strike up a conversation with the person at the next table, who turns out to be a new business owner. He says "can you help me with my corporate documents?" You say "Sure."

"Oh, and I can use an update to my Trust too."

"Sounds good. Here's my business card."

Later, you have a long meeting with him in your office and gather all of the information you need (he can't email it to you because email doesn't exist yet, and it's too many pages to send by fax).

You then spend the rest of the day dictating the contents of the documents into your tape recorder, your secretary spends the next day typing it up and hands you a draft. You then redline the draft and hand it back to your secretary, they revise it, and so on. You send the client a bill at the end of the month for "legal services" in the amount of $3,000 because that seems about fair.

Those days are long gone.

Now there are too many lawyers and they are not chosen based on the quality of their work. They are chosen based on their marketing value. Young associates don't become partners based on their commitment to the firm, they become partners based on the clients they can bring in and their billable hours. So why care about the quality of the work?

Innovation and nimbleness allow lawyers to do better quality work at one-tenth the price, but something has been lost over the years and it needs to be revived in the practice of law. Lawyers need to be able to learn what high quality work looks like.

The quality of your work matters. Whatever your career goal – to grow a solo practice, to become partner in a firm, etc. – this book will help you. And, since the quality of your life matters too, and directly impacts your work, we will explore ways to be a more relaxed, confident, and happy lawyer who has a reputation to be proud of.

This book will not teach you how to make money as a lawyer. Law is an industry, and like any industry, to make money requires good office politics, marketing strategies, and a host of other skills. But the quality of your work and the attitude you bring to it are the foundation for those other skills.

The stories of young lawyers crying in their cars every day on the way to work are true. The rate of burnout and substance abuse among lawyers, young and old, is extraordinarily high. There are many contributors to these problems, some from within and some from outside the legal industry.

But a big contributor is the feeling that success in litigation is a crapshoot. As a result, lawyers lose a sense of control over their cases and a resulting loss of a sense of control over their lives.

I hope this book can address that. I also hope to fill a hole that many young lawyers identify in their legal education – that law school teaches thinking and theories but does not teach you how to practice law. Your legal education gave you the building blocks you need, but being a good litigator requires you to assemble these blocks, and this book can help.

Whether you are going off on your own or starting as an associate in a law firm, this book will share some of the lessons, techniques, and wisdom that we have learned. These are lessons that no law school or senior partner will teach you; lessons that will allow you to quickly win more cases, advance your career, and avoid burnout. And if you are a more experienced lawyer, I hope there are a few lessons in here that make you say "I never thought of that!"

INTRODUCTION

THE SECRET TO LITIGATION

The Tale of the Lost Adventurers

"There once were two adventurers who found themselves lost in the forest.

After days of wandering, they stumbled across a tall stone wall. They followed the wall around, but there was no entrance.

Climbing up a nearby tree, they could see that the wall enclosed a paradise: endless fruit trees and fresh running water.

The wall was easy enough to climb, so the first traveler climbed up and over.

The second returned to the forest to find other lost adventurers."

> *"Can you imagine what I would do if I could do all I can?"*
>
> *– Sun Tzu*

To understand litigation, you must start with the basics.

Lawsuits provide a direct avenue to petition a branch of government to do something, or to order someone to do something. This is the closest that most people will have to direct control over government. It is even far greater control for any single person than voting. For that reason, it makes sense that the legal system is complicated and often feels like wading through quicksand.

Because of this complexity, new lawyers have always felt lost. This was true sixty years ago when they were thrown into trial after two weeks on the job, and this was true ten years ago when they were given thousands of pages of discovery to review without any guidance. And today, new lawyers are at a larger disadvantage than ever.

Some people compare litigation to war: it's time consuming, messy, expensive, and stressful. There are usually two adverse sides, and, after a trial, one will be declared the victor. This is probably the worst analogy for litigation, and those stuck in this anachronistic description do themselves – and their clients – a disservice.

Introduction

Others say litigation is like chess: a battle of minds and wills. This too is an imperfect analogy. In chess, unlike litigation, each player begins on equal footing. Further, chess has no middle ground. Although the players can reach a stalemate, there is no outcome where one player ends up slightly ahead and the other slightly behind. Chess also does not offset a win or loss by the amount of time remaining on the clock, whereas a lawsuit outcome is offset by the amount of money and time spent or saved.

There are countless other imperfect analogies: poker, medicine, car repair, plumbing, racketeering, or policework. I have even heard a lawyer once compare litigators to priests.

But litigation is so complex and varied that it's a mistake to compare it to something else. That's not to say that a lawyer is completely unlike a soldier, or that war and chess strategies are inapplicable. Nonetheless, it's better to compare those things to litigation rather than the other way around.

Poker is like litigation because you have to work with what you have and strategic bluffing is important…

Medicine is like litigation because you have to accurately diagnose the problem to cure it…

Plumbing is like litigation because you have to clean up someone else's… mess.

The secret to litigation is not to approach it like a battle, or approach it like chess, or approach it like something else. Rather, litigation has to be understood in its own right.

If I had to summarize the secret to litigation in one word, it is "balance." Litigation requires you to balance assertiveness with non-assertiveness, objectiveness with subjectiveness, openness with deception. And just like a gymnast, who has to constantly shift postures to stay upright, the center of gravity in a lawsuit shifts depending on the circumstances and you have to adapt to remain in balance. If your approach to a lawsuit is out of balance, you will face problems very quickly and you won't know why. You will blame everyone and everything: your client, the judge, opposing counsel, your staff, and the system. This will lead to poor results and burnout.

This book is divided into four parts, which build on each other:

The first adjusts your attitude: you must have the right mental foundation upon which to build. These are principles that can apply to your life, not just your practice.

The second teaches skills that will directly improve your work. This part of the book also goes into detail on techniques to improve your case management and big-picture skills.

The third provides the next-level insights that allow you to see your case from above and make smart strategic decisions. Knowing the motivations that drive cases toward settlement, the emotional value of your client's claims, the personality types you will encounter, and how to leverage "keystones" will take you from good to great and give you the ability to predict and control outcomes.

Introduction

The fourth and final part of the book discusses specific strategies that you can apply to your cases. It also provides guidance as to when and how to apply them, their strengths and weaknesses, and their counters.

To use an imperfect analogy: if learning law was like building a structure, then traditional law school classes would be the raw material, practical classes would be the construction skills, and this book would be the blueprints.

The practical advice in this book does not require you to practice law in an ideal world where your clients tell you everything, your budget is unlimited, opposing counsel is reasonable (or coherent), and the judge has time to thoroughly analyze your case.

This book applies to you: the modern practitioner of the legal arts, whose clients fall behind on their bills, who has cases that lack necessary pieces of crucial evidence, and who appears regularly before judges who don't have time to fully consider the arguments or spend more than five minutes to hear an important motion.

In the spirit of balance, each chapter begins with a zen-like story and a Sun Tzu quote. I did not make up the zen-like stories, but adapted ancient stories to modern times. You will also come across "True Stories," which should be understood to be "mostly" true stories. I changed them a little to anonymize them and more succinctly make the point they are supposed to make. Lastly, I encourage you to do the Exercises, which were designed to help you internalize the lessons.

SKIPPING THE LEARNING CURVE

Because of the way of things, the practice of law may often seem like a mystery to you. There is a steep learning curve, and many lawyers don't know how to progress along it. Yet, even with all of the real-world hurdles, you can do better.

This book teaches you how.

PART I

ATTITUDE ADJUSTMENT

The Tale of the Dart Thrower

"A young man heard about an old veteran who was hanging out at the local bar and beating everyone at darts.

The young man was arrogant and an expert dart thrower, so he went to the bar to challenge the vet.

He threw three darts in a row, each one a bullseye. 'Ha! Top that old man!' He said to the vet.

The vet calmly put a chair on top of the bar top at the other end of the room, stood on top of the chair, and, while the entire place stood in hushed silence, threw a bullseye.

The young man shook as he climbed up on the bar top and could not bring himself to ascend the chair or even throw a dart while precariously standing on the bar top.

'Young man,' the vet said, 'you may have bravado and the talent to throw a dart, but you do not have the mental discipline to be a champion.'"

> *"If the mind is willing, the flesh could go on and on without many things."*
>
> *— Sun Tzu*

As lawyers, we often face conflicts, ethical dilemmas, and seemingly no-win situations. Many important decisions are made during times of stress or exhaustion, when we are not at our best. These choices have consequences, putting you and your client on a path that may not lead where you want to go. No one can predict the future, and no one will make the right decision every time, but having a carefully considered set of values that informs your professional decisions will help you with these challenging moments.

These values are different than the Rules of Professional Conduct that are issued by the Bar of your State. The Rules provide strict guidance regarding actions. Having the right values, on the other hand, will create a mindset that leads naturally to the kind of actions you want to take. This is helpful in "gray area" situations where the law and the ethical rules won't tell you what to do – with the right underlying mindset, you're more likely to make the right choice on your own.

Attitude Adjustment

But the right attitude is also important at other times. Taking an action only because it is required by the law or ethical rules will come across to others differently than taking the same action because you honestly want to do the right thing. You can behave ethically, respectfully, and professionally, but if you have an underlying attitude of contempt, impatience, or superiority, it will shine through. Clients, opposing counsel, judges, and juries will respond to your attitude and not your words, leaving you confused when you get the wrong results even though you did the "right" thing.

This list of values is the one I try to work by. Some of these have helped me avoid costly mistakes; others arose out of prior mistakes. They have evolved over time, and will continue to evolve. At the end of the day, it is up to you to choose the values that you work (and live) by. I am offering mine only as an example. If it is helpful, feel free to adopt it, if not, toss it out. But remember that we're all living by a set of values, we just don't always know what they are. Bringing yours into awareness, where you can evaluate and adjust them to help you reach the outcomes you want, is one of the most valuable exercises you can do, not just in your legal career, but in your life.

•

HUMILITY

•

Humility will improve every aspect of your practice. If you adopt it as a general attitude, and not just a professional attitude, it will also improve your relationships, your leisure activities, and your general satisfaction and contentment.

Humans have a tendency away from humility. We all want our friends, family, colleagues, and clients to think the best of us. At times, we all feel like we are the star of our own movie. As attorneys, we face huge pressure to attract clients, impress partners, and intimidate opposing counsel in a competitive business environment. Humility seems like the opposite of what we need in order to accomplish those goals. After all, your business depends on your ability to sell yourself and fight for your clients.

But true humility is not timidity or a reflection of low self-esteem. We are all better at some things and worse at others, we all have more gifts in some areas and less in others, and we are all more alike than we are different — humility remembers that. Humility means that you do not feel superior to other people, but you do not feel inferior, either. Rather, you know you can learn something from everyone you meet. We are all taking turns being the hero, the villain, and the comic relief in each other's stories; humility lets you take a deep breath, relax, and surrender the role of the judge.

Humility makes you:

- Careful and focused in your work, because you are comfortable with the idea that you are human and you make mistakes just like everyone else. In a law practice, this means doing your research even when you think you know the answer, giving documents one more read-through, and asking a few more questions to make sure you understand what someone is trying to tell you.

- Curious, because you know that you don't know everything, and there is always more to learn. In a law practice, this means intentionally looking at your case from other points of view, getting to know your clients and colleagues as people, constantly seeking out other perspectives, learning about things that are outside your area of expertise, and asking questions.

- Compassionate with others and yourself, because you remember that we all have good and bad moments and good and bad days, and that doesn't define who we are. In a law practice, this means being patient with difficult people, making a point of seeing difficult behavior as a symptom and not a personality, moving forward with a productive and problem-solving attitude when someone makes a mistake, taking appropriate responsibility when you make a mistake, offering help when you can, and asking for help when you need it.

- Flexible, because your way isn't the only way. In a law practice, this means adjusting your communication style to match the people you're talking to, being creative and collaborative in discovery disputes and negotiations, exploring more than one solution to difficult situations, and always looking for and considering alternative approaches.

Courage

We all want to be more confident. It comes easily to some of us; not so easily to others. If you're not confident but you want to look that way, there are hundreds of helpful articles about how to do it – stand up straight, take up space, dress the part, don't let your voice lilt up at the end of a sentence, and so on. But is confidence really what we need?

Ironically, people who have less information tend to be more confident about their choices. Overconfidence reliably leads to bad decisions and poor outcomes. Although confidence will let you face obstacles fearlessly, it won't necessarily help you overcome them or excel in your career.

In reality, we are all going to face situations where we feel afraid, insecure, or overwhelmed, and we will keep facing those situations as long as we keep learning and progressing. Confidence can make you feel comfortable in those situations, but it can also make you careless and unprepared. Instead of confidence, what you need is courage.

Courage makes you:

- Comfortable with discomfort, because you know it is a natural part of life that you have encountered before and will encounter again. In a law practice, this means being willing to do things that are outside your comfort zone even though you feel afraid. For some lawyers, this might mean facing a fear of public speaking, for others it might mean listening to an emotional client instead of changing the subject, for others it might mean fighting for a cause.

- Willing to do what needs to be done to overcome obstacles, because you know that although you are not prepared, you can become prepared if you work hard. In a law practice, this means spending extra time on a brief, an argument, or a negotiation strategy so you are as prepared as you can be, and working intentionally on your weak skills by taking classes, reading books, and learning from people you admire.

- A smart risk taker, because you aren't paralyzed by fear of failure or blinded by overconfidence. In a law practice, this means looking at issues from every angle so you know as many options and potential outcomes as you can, listening to your fear and self-doubt without being ruled by them, and constantly questioning the things you feel certain about.

HONESTY

Everyone tells a "white lie" at times. As a lawyer, you will encounter many instances of "untruths":

- Your client lies about the strength of the case, and you find yourself facing a very different set of facts once you review the documents.

- Your client's former lawyer glossed over the potential expense of the lawsuit in order to get the case, and now the case is unfinished and they're in a messy fee dispute.

- Your eight-year-old lies about how she's doing in school, and you have an embarrassing conference with the teacher.

Lying, misleading, and omitting important information is so natural that people do it without even thinking. But eliminating as much of it as possible from your legal practice will make you a better lawyer and prevent problems.

Lying is hard work: you have to make it convincing; you have to remember it; you might even have to make up more lies in order to maintain it. Every lie you tell is a thing your brain must keep track of, and there are only so many things a person can juggle at once. By having a general rule that you don't lie, you force yourself to consider the cost and benefit of every lie you choose to tell.

If honesty is your general rule:

- You won't mislead in order to get work. In your law practice, this means being open with clients about the cost of moving forward, the potential outcomes, and the risks, even when that might mean they choose a different lawyer or decide not to go forward at all. But a client who doesn't hire you because you told the truth is a client who will be unhappy with your services when the truth inevitably comes out and could end up suing you over an unexpected bad outcome. A client who goes in with eyes open will be easier and more pleasant to work with.

- You will be persuasive without being misleading. In your law practice, this means taking all the facts, law, and evidence into account when you make arguments, dealing with unfavorable information head on instead of hiding it, and conceding weak arguments when you can. Taking this more objective approach to persuasion will make your strong arguments even stronger, because you aren't losing credibility by taking things out of context, ignoring bad facts, or pretending that there is only one side to the story. You will seem (and be) more trustworthy, and your reputation will benefit.

- You will navigate the gray areas gracefully, always remembering the value of silence. In your law practice, this means knowing when it is necessary and ethical to hide information, and when it is not necessary or not ethical. Your client will certainly have secrets that you must keep, but remember that most information will eventually come out. Keeping your client's secrets in the least dishonest way possible will preserve your credibility later.

LEARNING MINDSET

Stand in the halls of any courthouse and you will hear lawyers complaining that the judge doesn't read the papers, you can't predict what will happen at trial, jurors are crazy, and so on.

In reality, most judges read the briefs, and most jurors do their best to make the right decision. But all they have to work with is what you give them.

If you are making your points briefly, clearly, and backing up your arguments with well-presented research, then you are equipping your decision maker to make the right decision.

If you find yourself losing motions or cases that you think you should win and moaning that you just can't predict the outcome, you don't have a judge or jury problem; you have a case evaluation problem. Blaming the decision maker will not help you improve.

Attitude Adjustment

Every time you want to blame the judge, turn the spotlight around and reflect on your case and your performance. Even if you were right and the judge made the wrong decision, you will improve your own skills by constantly asking how you could have done better. If you find that the problems were with your case and not your performance, you will have improved your ability to predict outcomes. If your judge or jury didn't understand you, you probably didn't communicate effectively; if they understood you and ruled against you anyway, you probably didn't evaluate your case effectively.

And remember that "don't blame" goes the other way too. When you get a big win, don't rush to "blame" your superior lawyering skills. Take some time to celebrate and then do the same process of reflection that you would apply to a loss to see what you did well, where you got lucky, and where you can improve for next time.

You might find that your big win could have actually been bigger.

Cultivating an improvement and learning mindset instead of a blame mindset makes you:

- Resilient, because any outcome, whether a win or a loss, is an opportunity to learn. In your law practice, this means more time spent in intentional reflection when you have a bad outcome, but less time wallowing and being undermined by self-doubt.

- A more accurate evaluator and advisor, because you can predict outcomes. In your law practice, this doesn't mean that you know what's going to happen 100% of the time, but it does mean that you feel comfortable exploring likely outcomes and advising clients about risk.

- A better and more flexible communicator, because you are constantly asking yourself how to get your point across so the other person understands it. In your law practice, this means letting go of any ideas about legal writing or argument that are holding you back and adjusting your approach to the person you're dealing with.

- Responsible, because you can't fall back on blame. In your law practice, this means that you will do your best and be prepared; you will take the time to make sure your client understands what you're doing and why; and when things don't go your way, you will face it gracefully.

- A lifetime learner, because you know better than to rely on time and experience alone to make you wise. In your law practice, this means that you seek out resources to learn the skills you need (books, videos, classes, workshops – whatever works best for you). It also means that you don't limit your learning to the specific law related skills required in your practice area. You might find that studying psychology makes you a better communicator, studying acting makes you a better presenter, or studying creative writing makes you a better overall writer.

●
INDEPENDENT JUDGMENT
●

Sometimes, our clients treat us like interchangeable mouthpieces, hired to take an order and relay a message. We have all run into that client who wants little more than our signature on their documents and a warm body to stand up in court. But your job as an advocate is to push back and question your clients' assumptions in order to help them make better decisions. As a lawyer, you are in a unique position to have witnessed different approaches to solving problems, and can, therefore, advise a client from a perspective they have never encountered.

It is natural to worry that disagreement will result in the client finding new counsel. And there is a risk that suggesting a strategy that goes awry will result in the blame being pointed in your direction. But if you have questions about a client's decision, it is for good reason, and you must raise your concerns. In most cases, a pushy client will appreciate your input even if they ultimately insist that you do things their way. When things go wrong, you will often get credit for providing good advice (trust me). Or, if it is a client with a short memory, you will have created a solid paper trail. If questioning a client's decisions gets you fired, that is a red flag revealing itself – you were better off not getting in any deeper with that client!

It can be extremely difficult to turn down a potentially good-paying client, especially when times are slow. But it is usually better for your health, wealth, and happiness to miss out on an opportunity than to take on the wrong client.

Using independent judgment will make you:

- Respectful of yourself and your profession, because you will use your knowledge, skills, and expertise every day. In your law practice, this means that you see yourself as an advisor and counselor who offers a valuable service, and you take the time to help your clients understand your role so you can give them what they need (even when it isn't what they think they need).

- Sleep better at night, because you don't take actions that you aren't comfortable with. In your law practice, this may mean turning down clients, saying no to clients, and occasionally losing clients, but more often it will mean talking issues out with them so you can find the right course of action together.

- More empathetic, because your judgment is only as good as your understanding of your client's situation. In your law practice, this means learning your client's needs, interests, and ultimate goals and mapping a route to reach those goals. Clients will treat you like the trusted advisor you are if they feel that you truly understand them.

•
PERSONAL WELL-BEING
•

The legal profession often seems to reward pushy, loud, aggressive, and unwavering behavior. And it definitely seems to reward around the clock work.

Attitude Adjustment

In addition, a lawyer's job is often to step into the shoes of clients who are angry, afraid, and facing serious consequences if the case doesn't go their way. You take on their conflict and fight for them. If you are working on contingency, you may have even more to lose than they do! On the other hand, if they are paying you by the hour, you struggle to do everything necessary to win the case while staying within their budget.

The fact that lawyers are required to take continuing legal education classes about substance abuse issues tells you everything you need to know about how stressful and all-consuming our profession is.

Sitting behind a computer screen under office lights for 14 hours a day is draining. It certainly isn't the best environment for staying physically fit and healthy. And, when your job primarily involves mental effort, it is easy to forget that your brain is part of your body, and it won't stay healthy if the rest of you doesn't.

You must take intentional steps to care for your physical, mental, and emotional well-being. How you do that depends on you. You might develop a hobby or interest, and schedule time for it every week or even every day. You might plan a morning or evening ritual that you find refreshing. You might join a gym, take up a sport, embrace a spiritual practice, or just walk around the block a few times each day to clear your head. But no matter what you do to maintain your health – relaxing hobbies, sports and exercise, strong relationships with family or friends, spiritual practices, therapy, etc. – it should be a priority in your life. And if you notice a change in how you feel, don't ignore it.

Taking care of your physical, mental, and emotional health will make you:

- Happier and more energetic, because you aren't stuck in an endless cycle of stress followed by sleep (rinse, repeat).

- Patient with clients, co-workers, and opposing counsel, because you are more relaxed. When you take care of yourself, you have more energy to take care of others. And when you make a point of finding ways to relax and de-stress, it is easier to put little things into perspective.

- Resilient, because taking care of yourself builds the resources you need to face big obstacles.

•
EMOTIONAL INTELLIGENCE
•

Lawyers work in conflict, where emotions run high and trust is at a minimum. We wouldn't be human if we didn't become, at times, emotionally involved in our cases. This can leave us feeling personally betrayed by opposing counsel, the judge, or even our own clients. I have witnessed multi-year long feuds between lawyers that have arisen from something as minor as a discovery dispute.

We will all, at some point, be furiously angry with a disrespectful opposing counsel, or completely blinded by our sympathy for a client. But unexamined reactions can lead to bad decisions, seep into the tone of written material, and unnecessarily damage relationships with clients, other lawyers, witnesses, and fact finders.

Attitude Adjustment

Emotion can be harnessed and used to great effect, but only if you learn to recognize it and use it intentionally. So get in touch with your feelings – they drive most of what we do, whether we know it or not. Your emotions make you care about your client and present her position persuasively. They can help you see things from other points of view, motivate you to work hard when you might otherwise give up, and provide the passion that makes you a compelling speaker. But most of us need intentional practice to use this powerful tool effectively.

Remember though: emotional intelligence is not only about being in touch with your own emotions, it is also about understanding the emotional state of others.

Building your emotional intelligence will make you:

- Persuasive, because understanding how you feel will help you present your story persuasively. In your law practice, this means remembering that you are always having emotional reactions, and those reactions are a source of information and power if you understand them.

- Empathetic, because your interest in your own emotional reactions makes you interested in other people's reactions. In your law practice, this means looking at your story from different points of view and approaching everyone – clients, witnesses, opposing counsel – with curiosity and a basic sense of goodwill and respect.

- A whole person, because you know we are all driven by emotion. In your law practice, this means that you don't feel like a superior rational being when your client reacts emotionally, and you don't assume that your view of things is entirely objective.

•

LIKE YOUR CLIENT

•

Some clients are difficult. But we are entrusted with the job of advocating for them and protecting them, and you must find something in them (or in their cause) to like, respect, identify with, or have compassion for.
If your client's personality is so terrible that you can't find any redeeming quality, you should probably pass on the case.

Some lawyers have a business model with the attitude of "piss on them, they hired me, they can pay my bills and get what they get." If your practice requires that attitude, find a way to change your practice or your outlook. Otherwise, you will burn out or become the kind of lawyer no one wants to be.

TIP

Don't be naïve. Even if you like your client, and they like you, you must always protect yourself. A lot of clients won't think twice about throwing you under the bus if they think it will improve their chances of winning. But it is your license on the line, so you must always retain the attributes of Courage and Independent Judgment.

Finding a way to like your clients will make you:

- Less likely to have a conflict with your client. No matter how good you think your acting skills are, most people can tell when you don't like them, and people who don't feel liked aren't going to be at their best in that relationship. In your law practice, this means getting to know your clients so you can find things to like and respect about them, and carefully examining your negative feelings to find and address their causes before they poison the relationship.

- More persuasive, because the fact that you like your client will shine through in your arguments, your writing, and your actions, and it is easier for a judge or jury to like your client when they see that you do too. In your law practice, this means considering your underlying attitude as an important ingredient in your work.

- Happier. If you find a way to like your clients, your work day will be more pleasant. Yes, you may take losses a little harder, but you'll feel even better about your wins. And you won't waste energy pretending you can tolerate people you actually can't stand.

- More energetic, because it is easier to work hard for someone you like. Law often requires long days and working on weekends, and that will be a lot less painful if you feel like you're doing it for someone you care about, and not just for the money.

IN SUMMARY

Think about your values and revisit them often.

Eight attributes that will help are:

- Humility
- Courage
- Honesty
- Having a learning mindset
- Independent judgment
- Maintaining your well-being
- Emotional intelligence
- Liking your client

These are the attributes that I try to nurture in my life and practice, but don't feel bound by these. If something isn't working, change it, adjust it, or throw it out and start over.

The goal is to develop guiding principles and priorities that make your work as satisfying and enjoyable as possible while helping you grow into the person you want to be.

PART II

BEYOND BASIC SKILLS

The Tale of the Three Friends

"Three friends had just finished hiking around a lake to hang out and relax.

The first stood up and said 'I forgot my towel,' and walked across the water to go back to the car and get her towel. She returned a few minutes later gingerly walking across the water with her towel.

The second stood up and said 'that reminds me, I forgot our cooler with our food.' He too walked across the water and returned shortly with the cooler.

The third stood up and said 'you're not the only ones that can do magic tricks' and ran to the lake. As soon as he stepped on the water, he fell in. Then he climbed out, soaking wet, and tried again. Over and over, he fell in the water.

As the other two watched, the first turned to the second and said 'do you think we should tell him where the sand bar is?'"

SKIPPING THE LEARNING CURVE

> *"He will win who, prepared himself, waits to take the enemy unprepared."*
>
> *— Sun Tzu*

Graduating from law school and passing the Bar proves that you have basic comprehension, writing, and speaking skills. You might be above average or even exceptional at one or all of these basic skills, and that's great, because these are the fundamental building blocks that you need as a litigator. And, if you think you could use some improvement (we can all use some improvement), there are hundreds of books, classes, videos, and other resources that can help you get better.

This section is about identifying skills that go beyond the basics. Master these, and you'll be excellent, not just competent.

This section also identifies some common mistakes and how to avoid making them.

If you (like most readers of this book) are a new lawyer, you probably worry about your lack of experience when talking to a new client or facing a very experienced opposing counsel. Or maybe you worry because you didn't go to a top law school, or because you've never done a trial. When you are up against lawyers who advertise their forty years of experience, thousands of cases settled, or hundreds of trials, it is easy to feel intimidated.

But no one becomes a great lawyer passively. Improvement comes only with active learning and analysis of your own performance. Although most people believe that a lawyer who has practiced for forty years must be better than a lawyer who has practiced for ten, this is often not true. Too many lawyers assume that they have become better lawyers because they have done it longer, or because they have handled more cases. But unless they have actively evaluated their performance along the way, they have not improved. You can "catch up" with (or easily exceed) many of your more experienced colleagues and opponents by actively working to improve crucial skills.

COMMON AND PERSISTENT MYTHS

Just like any profession, there are a number of myths that exist in the legal industry. Identifying these will prevent you from being intimidated and also will encourage you to continue learning.

THE RANDOM OUTCOME MYTH

A lot of lawyers believe that the outcome of a lawsuit is random. They will repeatedly state "well, you can't know how a judge or jury will go, so I will present my best case, they will give theirs, and then it's 50-50." But these same lawyers will say that a client is better off retaining them over a competitor because they are "a better lawyer." If outcomes were truly random, then the quality of the lawyer would not matter.

The truth is that the quality of the lawyer matters a lot, and litigation outcomes are not random. While there is always a risk that a judge or jury will surprise you, if you are a good lawyer (and follow the advice in this book), a surprise outcome will not be frequent. That doesn't mean that every case is "winnable" (although, this largely depends on the definition of "win," as discussed later in Part III). It just means that the likely range of outcomes is predictable and a good lawyer is able to move the actual outcome to a more favorable result.

THE EXPERIENCE/SUCCESS MYTH

It is easy to believe that the number of years as a lawyer matters. And it does "matter," but not to the degree that people want to believe. Like practicing an instrument or a sport, there are distinct skills that must be developed. And just like an instrument or a sport, unless you specifically work on practicing those skills, you will not improve. The vast majority of these skills do not improve much from passively using them. For instance, you may become a slightly better writer by drafting discovery responses or motions over twenty years, but you will not become great unless you are able to identify your weaknesses and fix them. A lawyer practicing for only five years, with drive and focus, can easily outperform lawyers that have been practicing for twenty, thirty, or forty years.

Just like any skill, you can improve much faster and further with a focused approach to improving and learning than a lifetime of doing things "the same way."

The Ivy League Myth

A similar Myth is that the ranking of a law school or law firm matters. This information is not conclusive; it is nothing more than another piece of data. The ranking of a school or law firm can never change the facts, evidence, or law. And even if a law school or firm is of "higher" quality, that doesn't mean the associated attorneys are improving over time. A lawyer with a learning mindset will become better no matter where they are educated or where they work, while a lawyer with a blame mindset will never improve at all.

Too many lawyers are self-conscious because of these myths. Don't let these myths cause you to be intimidated, for instance by the stature of opposing counsel. But also, don't let these myths cause you to have a false sense of security, for instance by working for a large law firm or graduating from a high-ranked school. You must approach each case on its own merit and to the best of your ability, without allowing these myths to affect your decision making, and you must always work to improve your own skills.

TIP

It is easy to be discouraged as a new lawyer. You will inevitably run into opponents that have more impressive credentials or marketing material, and your peers or bosses may express the opinion that litigation is a crap-shoot.

But these myths are just that: myths. If you focus on learning and improving the quality of your work, better results will follow.

GATHERING THE RIGHT INFORMATION

At the start of any case, it is important to gather the right information, and in the right way. Knowing your case, the judge, and the witnesses will lay the groundwork for your preparation and strategy implementation.

KNOW YOUR CASE

Doesn't it sound obvious? Of course, you have to know your case! But it is easy to get lost in all the things that seem more urgent – pleadings, discovery, client management – and assume that you are learning your case as you go along.

It is easy to default into a habit-driven mindset:

> *step 1 - file a demurrer*
> *step 2 - serve interrogatories*
> *steps 3-7 - do what I always do*
> *step 8 - review everything right before trial*

But taking intentional steps to become familiar with the facts, evidence, and law underlying your arguments will pay off at every stage. And learning your case with an objective and neutral mindset will allow you to see the weaknesses and address them.

The keys to learning your case are to start right away, review and update often, and stay organized. Make the process streamlined by creating an index of the documents, caselaw, and statutes. Address and evolve these indices as the case progresses.

From day one, maintain a deposition outline for each potential witness that you work on *as the case develops*, instead of waiting until the day before a deposition to put it together. Likewise, from day one, maintain outlines for motions-in-limine and your closing argument.

Another useful tool to help you stay on top of your case is a timeline that you create when you first talk to your client and that you update periodically as you gather more information. If you keep your timeline updated, you'll find that it is an incredibly valuable resource when you can't remember a fact, need to find a piece of evidence, or have to figure out where new information fits into the story.

It is easy to put much of this work off until later, because there is always something more urgent to do and clients are often reluctant to pay for a lot of lawyer hours right away, but if you do as much of this preparation as early as you can, you will save time in the long-run. Sometimes, a client's budget just won't allow it; in those circumstances, it can be worth putting in a few "no-charge" hours or agreeing to a flat fee for some of these early tasks. Every minute you put in to organize and get to know your case early saves you time and headaches later on.

The value of learning and organizing every detail of the case cannot be overstated.

SKIPPING THE LEARNING CURVE

TRUE STORY

Before filing the complaint in a professional liability case against an insurance broker, we did a detailed analysis. Besides the obvious causation issue, we also discovered a damages issue due to the nitty-gritty of how insurance policies pay out. On face value, the damages could have been high, but only a deeper analysis revealed that our client could easily win the case and get almost no damages due to his unique circumstances.

The defendant was represented by a big firm that we knew operated a "Delegation Model" (which is described in Part III). I called opposing counsel, who turned out to be very smart and very friendly.

I said "look, I know that we have causation problems because of X, Y, and Z, so maybe we can work out a quick settlement before both sides get too deep into this." He was on board since I acknowledged the liability problems. Implementing a Decoy strategy (which described in Part IV), I kept the negotiations focused on the causation and liability elements. I was gambling that because opposing counsel was smart and also because of the use of the Delegation Model, that he had not taken the time to do a detailed analysis of the damages, and would take it on face value without getting into the weeds on it.

The gamble paid off, and we were able to settle quickly. Opposing counsel thought he had done a great job since the amount was so much "lower" than the "potential upside" at trial. He never realized that we ended up settling for about double our true potential upside at trial.

Know Your Judge

When I graduated law school, my father bought me a novelty T-shirt that had the phrase "a good lawyer knows the law, a great lawyer knows the judge." While the implication is that a lawyer will get special treatment if they are friends with the judge (a sentiment that is not true; you are more likely to get extra scrutiny), there is another interpretation: a great lawyer has investigated the judge, and has some insight about the judge.

Judges are people too! Learning what your judge is like – personality, temperament, experience, writing style – will help you tailor your arguments directly to your judge and also formulate a better case strategy.

But don't worry if you have never been in front of your judge before. Ask lawyer friends who might have been in front of your judge, read reviews and other information online, and see if your judge posts tentative decisions. If the tentative decisions are easily accessible, there is no better way to get to know your judge than to read how he or she has ruled in other cases. You'll learn what cases your judge likes to cite, how your judge analyzes issues, and whether your judge issues discovery sanctions.

TIP

Maintain a document for each judge that you're in front of where you keep notes about the judge. While reading tentative rulings, if the judge cites cases paste those citations into your notes, along with the judge's use of them. Nothing is more persuasive to a judge than to see her own most-referenced cases cited by counsel.

Pay attention while you're waiting in court, too – while you're waiting for your case management conference to be heard, you can learn a lot about a judge's temperament by watching him or her interact with other lawyers and the rulings in other cases. This will give you a lot of information about the judge, such as whether they prefer a formal or informal demeanor from their lawyers.

Some specific items you should look for:

- The level of analysis in the judge's tentative rulings. You should favor judges that give detailed and well-reasoned rulings over those that just give a cursory sentence about how they're going to rule. At the very least, if you lose a motion, it is more satisfying to understand a judge's reasoning than to be left in the dark.

- The judge's views on discovery sanctions. You should always assume that if you don't have enough evidence to win at the start of the case, it will be hard to get the evidence you need (and you might not be able to). If you need evidence from your opponent, you should favor judges who are not hesitant to issue discovery sanctions. You will need the teeth of sanctions to get your evidence. Conversely, if your client is going to be difficult, you don't want a judge who is willing to give heavy sanctions.

- The judge's frequency of granting summary judgment. This datapoint can be vastly different depending on the cases a particular judge hears, so it is not as useful as a lot of people believe. And you should not be surprised if your judge grants nearly 70% of summary judgment motions that they hear: a summary judgment motion is a very expensive undertaking, so it self-selects for stronger motions. But it can still be helpful to know if your judge's summary judgment rate is near 0 or 100%, which may indicate a bias towards or against granting these dispositive motions.

SKIPPING THE LEARNING CURVE

TRUE STORY

We were defending a case involving a complicated landlord-tenant dispute. From the beginning, the plaintiff's counsel insisted that they would file a motion for summary judgment. After months of litigation, the plaintiff's counsel made a settlement demand and said "we're about to file our MSJ, so keep in mind that you're going to have a lot of work if you don't accept."

I checked the court's reservation system and saw that the first available MSJ slot was two months after our scheduled trial day.

As a result, plaintiff's counsel was unable to get a hearing for their MSJ. The judge, in denying their ex-parte request to advance the hearing date, said "you snooze you lose" (not in so many words).

You can guess how the settlement discussions shifted.

This is an important lesson to remember! Courts are often very busy. In departments that require a hearing reservation, make sure that you reserve a motion for summary judgment date early if you think there's a chance that you might bring one.

Otherwise, the only available hearing date might be after trial and not every judge will be sympathetic if you drafted your motion but were unable to get a date because you did not reserve one when you had the chance.

For these same reasons, you should not postpone discovery. Start early!

KNOW YOUR WITNESSES

Sometimes, as we craft the most persuasive arguments, refine our stories, and organize our documents, we lose sight of the (sometimes terrifying) fact that most of this information will be expressed through witnesses.

Preparing them to testify, and preparing yourself to interact with them productively, is essential. Even if your case has little chance of going to trial, any witness who will testify at deposition or trial has the power to make or break your case. And the most important thing to remember as you prepare your witnesses is that they are human: testifying at a deposition or in court is not something they do (or want to do) every day, and your job is to make their job easy.

What is easy for a witness? Telling a story that fits their authentic memory of the events. I intentionally did not say "telling the truth," because people's memories are complicated and two witnesses can each firmly believe that their very different memories are the truth. But whatever your witness actually thinks will come out if they are subjected to long or intense questioning, so you must work with it. It is your job to craft a theory that fits the witnesses' testimony; it is not the witnesses' job to alter their story to fit your theory. That's why you need to have your witnesses in mind at every stage of your preparation – it is a problem to have a legal theory that can't accommodate a certain fact that one of your witnesses believes. You don't have full control over that witness, and that testimony could become a gaping hole in your story. Even if the offending fact is completely irrelevant, it's probably going to come out and it is up to you to make it fit by adapting your theory to it, not the other way around.

Preparing Your Case – The Theory, The Story, and The Theme

As a lawyer, you wear a lot of hats. You are a scholar, a writer, a counselor, an advocate, a public speaker, an analyzer of numbers and evidence... Sometimes, you might perform all of these jobs in a single day. But one of your most important jobs is one you might not spend much time thinking about: you are a storyteller.

Stories are compelling and comforting. We listen to them automatically, conditioned to do so by the bedtime stories of childhood and the books, movies, and TV shows we turn to for entertainment as adults. Because we have so much experience consuming stories, we intuitively understand their structure – a story that proceeds from beginning to end in the usual way is believable because it fits into our existing mental map, and a well-timed disruption to a predictable story grabs our attention and sticks in our memories. As a lawyer, you are telling an unusual story – one where your audience has the power to write the ending. You have to make sure that the only satisfying resolution to that story is one that benefits your client.

Law school probably did a good job giving you the skills to figure out the "theory" of your case – the logic by which your client prevails. But there is a lot more to your case than logic. Even a strong legal argument can fail if the outcome you're asking for doesn't seem fair. And people – even judges – determine "fairness" based on the whole story, and not a rigid calculation.

Keep notes on each witness from the start of the case – how were they involved, what are they like, what questions will you want to ask them, what documents do you want to put in front of them, where do they fit in your timeline, how will they look at their deposition or in front of a jury? Talk to them before you actually need to. Consider an in-person meeting, not just a phone call – some of these questions can only be answered if you are face to face. With respect to opposing witnesses, who you can't just have an informal talk with, ask your client and your witnesses to give you as much information as they can about what these people are like so you know how to communicate with them when you eventually get into a deposition.

By keeping this in mind all along, you increase the chance that you'll make the crucial connections that can make or break your overall strategy and create a story that holds up in deposition and in trial.

IN SUMMARY

Start your case preparation immediately. It will save your client a lot of money in the long run and get better results down the road if, at the beginning, you:

- Know your case by starting to prepare early.

- Know your judge by watching and listening in court (since you're there anyway), speaking with other lawyers, and reading tentative decisions.

- Know your witnesses and craft a legal theory that fits their authentic testimony.

That's not to say that the logic is irrelevant (more on this later). But people will resist an approach that asks them to disregard that story in favor of a logic puzzle. This is true even if the logic is irrefutable.

And while your case boils down to a formula – prove the elements of your case, rebut theirs – that is a deceptively simple way to look at it. After all, many stories are "formulaic." The main character fights the bad guy and wins, the flawed hero faces a big obstacle and grows, or the villain sets out to destroy the world but learns to love it instead. In law, a basic knowledge of the formula won't make your story great if you don't have the rest of the ingredients.

The key to winning – whether that is a single motion or a case through a favorable settlement or judgment – is to have a *believable* and *memorable* story that *fits your theory*. Most lawyers have made it a habit to focus their litigation approach on one or two of those three key ingredients. That is, perhaps they focus on believability but it's not memorable. Or they get bogged down in the theory and present a dry analysis that is poorly understood by the listener and quickly forgotten.

Get all three key ingredients right in your story and you will cook a winning recipe.

> **TIP**
>
> Litigation can be overwhelming, with one deadline after another and never enough time (or budget) to do everything you want to do to win your case. But don't fall into the trap of short-term thinking. Even if you are 99% sure that your case will settle, you will be better situated for that settlement if you start preparing your trial notebook early. This ensures that, if your case doesn't settle, you will be ready for trial. It also refines your storytelling by forcing you to think about your opening, closing, and the overall theme early in the case. Lastly, it informs your discovery plan, and ultimately strengthens your negotiating position.

Creating your theory, story, and theme

The theory, story, and theme are reliant on each other. Developing them is a recursive process – as you change one, the other two need to change as well. This can be a frustrating process, but if you approach it in an organized manner, the result will be worth the effort.

Develop your theory by looking at the jury instructions

The theory is how the evidence proves the facts and how the facts prove the legal elements of your case (or if you are representing the defendant, how the facts disprove an element of the plaintiff's case or proves an affirmative defense). You are already familiar with this from law school.

SKIPPING THE LEARNING CURVE

For instance, "when defendant failed to deliver the oranges, he breached the contract." Your theory should incorporate and address the opposing side's theory as well. For example, if the defense is "the oranges were not delivered because the contract called for plaintiff to pick them up," you cannot charge headlong into the case with your original theory that the defendant was in breach for failure to deliver the oranges (obviously this depends on the language of the contract, the interactions of the parties, etc.).

A lot of lawyers will get bogged down in a theory that doesn't fit the facts. In the above example, too many lawyers would try to squeeze a winning theory out of defendant's failure to deliver. Even if some argument can be made based on other facts of the case, it may be better to stop the mental gymnastics, relax your brain, and come up with a new theory.

The best place to begin developing your theory is by looking at the jury instructions. Often, the jury instructions will also provide useful comments and references to applicable case-law and statutes. By starting with the jury instructions, you are also getting pointed in the right direction for your research.

Once you identify all potential jury instructions, write out your theory in your trial notebook. Revisit and refine this theory as the litigation unfolds.

In order to develop a strong theory, you must have a solid conceptual understanding of the differences between evidence, facts, rules, and legal conclusions. Often, something can fall into more than one of these categories, but if you do not have a strong understanding of the four key parts of your case, then you will not develop a crystalized theory.

These parts are best understood from the legal conclusion backwards:

- **Legal conclusion:** this is the end result after you apply the facts to the rules. For instance, in the above breach of contract for the delivery of oranges, the legal conclusion is either "defendant breached the contract" or "defendant did not breach the contract."

- **Rules:** these are the elements and sub-elements that you need to prove, disprove, or prevent from being proven in order to reach the legal conclusion that you want. One rule for a breach of written contract requires that the parties have entered into a written contract. In turn, there is another relevant rule that if a contract is written, some parol evidence will be inadmissible if the agreement is fully integrated. You determine the potentially relevant rules by the facts available.

- **Facts:** these are an interpretation of evidence, and may or may not also be legal conclusions. For instance, "defendant signed the agreement" or "the parties entered into an integrated agreement" are both facts, but proving whether an agreement is integrated is also a legal conclusion reliant on its own sub-rules and sub-facts. Likewise, whether a certain mark constitutes a "signature" can itself be a legal conclusion reliant on its own subset of rules and facts. Unless accepted by the other side as true for the case, facts must be supported or disproved by the evidence.

- **Evidence:** this is the library of items that you can point to in order to craft the facts. For instance, the contract itself.

Many lawyers develop their theory at the start of the case and never change it, no matter what the evidence may show. Instead, they ignore evidence that does not fit into their theory and over-rely on evidence that is not as strong as they make it seem. As a result, they end up forced to craft a story that is not believable. Your theory must be comprehensive and you must revisit it regularly throughout the course of the lawsuit.

Develop your story by incorporating the bad facts, evidence, and law into the good facts, evidence, and law

From the start of your case think about all the "ingredients" you have in terms of a story:

- **The Characters:** The characters of your story are your client, the other party, and the witnesses. Do they fit easily and favorably into a hero/villain story? Don't assume that they do! If your client is unlikable, he won't be a believable hero, and if the other party is likeable, she won't be a believable villain. That's not a problem, it's an opportunity to create more complex roles that truly fit the people you're working with. Work with what you have, not what you want to have.

- **The Plot:** You'll find the plot in your timeline (which you will update as you gather evidence). You can't do much to alter the plot, but you can use it to structure a strong story. You want your story to be easily consistent with every item in the timeline that is undisputed. As for disputed items, try to create a story that explains them.

Think about all the times and places where you will have a chance to present your story over the course of your case. Obviously, you will present your story at trial and in any motions you file, but you will also present your story at other times.

For example, you will present your story at mediation, you will present your story at your client's deposition (although your client will do most of the presenting), and you will present your story in a more limited format at any deposition you take (through the questions you ask). So you might look at your case and decide that your major storytelling opportunities will be deposition, motion for summary judgment, mediation, and trial, and you will have minor storytelling opportunities at a few smaller motions and in your conversations with opposing counsel. Think about how you will present your story at each of these "stages."

Each stage has an audience: judge, jury, mediator, arbitrator, insurance company, opposing counsel, opposing party, maybe even the press, depending on what type of case you're dealing with. You will be presenting your story to some or all of them over the course of your case, and it is important to be able to tailor the story to each of them. In tailoring your story, you are presenting the same facts and evidence, but with different emphasis. As you get to know your audience, you will start to see which parts of the story are most likely to have an impact on them, and what storytelling style works best for them.

Although the underlying ingredients should be consistent from stage to stage, your story will change if you change your theory or discover new evidence. And even if everything else stays the same, your story should not necessarily remain unchanged if you think of a better story that fits the facts, evidence, and law.

Be flexible, and match your storytelling as much as possible to the audience's needs, preferences, and personalities if you want to be persuasive. A story focused on law, facts, and elements might be more persuasive to a judge ruling on summary judgment than a jury considering your case at trial; whereas a story humanizing your client might cause a jury to understand your case better than an academic recitation of legal elements.

For example, you might tell a judge that "Jack ascended the beanstalk." But you might tell opposing counsel that "Jack climbed up the vine, which happened to be a beanstalk." And you might tell a jury that "Jack, a wild-eyed teenager, came upon a giant beanstalk that reached into the heavens. Wild-eyed teenage boys being what they are, he then disregarded his own safety and climbed it."

All three examples tell the same story, but with a different emphasis and style.

A good way to figure out what kind of communication works for people is to pay attention to how they communicate with you. People tend to prefer to be communicated to in the same way that they communicate. Purposely reflecting the person you are communicating with can be extremely effective, as can purposely communicating in a way that makes them uncomfortable. Just like any speech, always consider your audience.

> **TIP**
>
> If you have the opportunity to watch a few trials, you should. It is absolutely astounding how lawyers try to paint their unsympathetic witness as a victim. Worse, when presented with a soft-spoken, likeable opposing party or witness, they will attack and villainize.
>
> Watch the jury's reaction: you will see eyebrows furrowed and heads tilted as they try to understand what it is that the lawyer sees that no one else does.
>
> Don't be that lawyer!

What belongs in your story?

Your story has two important goals. First, it must *believably* address your theory (and by necessity, it must also address your opponent's theory). Second, it must be *memorable*.

Don't ignore the bad facts, evidence, and law in developing your story! A frequent error that lawyers make is to never ever admit or acknowledge a bad fact. They justify this by saying "the other side has to make their own argument, I won't make it for them. I will set forth my best argument only, they will set forth their best argument only, and then it's a coin flip."

They are wrong. Ignoring bad facts, evidence, or law will make your story less believable. You want your story to incorporate (and not "spin") the bad things, not ignore them!

It is even better if you can transform your "bad facts" into facts that support your case. Don't create basic excuses for the bad items either. Spend time thinking about the bad parts and figuring out ways to make those things help your case.

And if the law isn't 100% on your side, face it head-on. Persuasive argument comes from telling a story that appears to have most likely happened. Every case has weaknesses, and if you acknowledge the weaknesses, then your story will be more believable. If your case had no weaknesses, then your opponent would give up unless they were completely in denial or incapable of reasoning. While you may encounter this opponent on occasion, it is not the norm. Most of the time, someone that seems to be in denial or incapable of reasoning understands your position but is doing a poor job of being persuasive and is pretending not to see any weaknesses in their own case.

You will be shocked at how often you will win even if (or rather because) you are admitting to more bad law or facts than your opponent.

If you have a choice between a simple story and a complicated one, choose the simpler story if you can. It will be easier to understand, more memorable, and more appealing than a fancier story. Always remember that a winning story is one that is *believable* and *memorable*.

TIP

A believable story that is not 100% in your favor is more persuasive than a story that is 100% in your favor but not likely to be believed.

Develop your theme

A good theme is the moral of the story. It persuades because it creates context for the evidence. Your theme is a repeating message that makes your story memorable and helps your decision maker come to the "right" conclusion. Persuasion is not about getting juries to remember what you say, it's about getting juries to believe that your story is more likely to be true, and therefore the outcome you are requesting is the proper outcome.

To craft a strong theme, think of it as a slogan: "If you do the work, you should get paid." Or it can be one word that summarizes what you want a jury to remember such as "late" (in a case where Defendant was running late and so he ran a red light causing an accident). You can even get inspiration from various movie catchphrases or lists of story themes. But above all else, make it simple, non-controversial, and easy to remember.

The theme has to arise out of the evidence and the story. Developing a specific catchphrase or slogan is not the goal (although often it will help serve to as a pneumonic device for the jurors to understand the case).

Rather, a theme is more conceptual. For instance, in the case of a Defendant running a red light, you can start your opening statement by saying "Late. Mr. Jones was late. He had a presentation to give and had already been reprimanded for his repeated tardiness." Or you can say "Mr. Jones was in a rush to get to work. He had a presentation to give and his boss was not going to be happy."

Both of these explain the theme of being late and help develop a motive for Mr. Jones running the red light. Of course, your story will obviously fall apart if Mr. Jones was not going to be late. But it will also not be believable if the presentation he was going to give was not important. For instance, if a defense witness is going to testify that "the presentation was not important; Mr. Jones could have given it at any time," then "late" might not be a good theme.

Here is a simple step-by-step technique to develop a strong theme:

- Brainstorm and write down ALL conclusions that can be drawn from the facts. Write the good and the bad.

- Write as many stories that you can think of that can be drawn from the facts. Do this for each conclusion that you brainstormed. Each story must incorporate all facts available. Don't worry about the specific language of the story or the believability. At this stage, you are just focused on getting every possible story written out that incorporates all of the facts. You should also not worry if you are making assumptions about facts and don't have evidence yet to support those assumed facts. Likewise, don't worry if some of the facts are disputed.

- Rank the stories on a scale of "strong," "medium," and "weak" for each of three categories: (a) fits the law, (b) on your side, and (c) believable.

- Pick the story that best fits the law AND is most on your side AND is most believable.

- Summarize the main point of the story in ONE sentence or less.

- Revisit at various points in the litigation. Focus your discovery efforts on establishing whether the assumed facts have evidence and whether there is evidence to support the disputed facts one way or the other.

- Narrow your stories as warranted until you are preparing for trial. You can only go to trial with a single story. Pick the one that best fits the law AND is most on your side AND is most believable. Picking the one story out of a handful that best meets these criteria is a judgment call that you will have to make. But if you have properly narrowed the stories down to a small list, any story you choose from that list will be the correct choice: there will almost never be "the perfect" story that fits all three criteria very well simultaneously.

IN SUMMARY

After gathering the information about your case, your judge, and the witnesses, you will be ready to prepare the cornerstones of your trial notebook:

- Theory.
- Story.
- Theme.

Too many lawyers skip this step, reasoning that they will do it after discovery and before trial.

Do not skip this step!

Developing these three elements early will guide and focus your discovery plan and negotiation strategy. You will have a better understanding of the strengths and weaknesses of your case.

Focus on two areas: believability/credibility, and memorability.

Make sure to revisit the theory, story, and theme as the case progresses because otherwise you will find yourself with a forgettable or not believable case.

Your Discovery Plan

Discovery can be boring, time consuming, and ultimately unproductive. It is the rare opponent who will send you the smoking gun document or make a truly damaging admission. But you can use the discovery process to get something more valuable: their theory, story, and theme.

Your goal in litigation is not to prove that they have "no case" (unless their case is truly frivolous). Your goal is to force them to argue their weakest story – that is, either a complex and forgettable story, or one that does not neatly fit their theory or the facts (or both).

Your opponent has a story and a theory even if they don't realize it, and even if they do a poor job of presenting it. Keep a file in which you draft your ideas of their theory, story, and theme. Draft all that come to mind. Then identify – within the document – which of these fit the law, which is most on their side, and which is most believable (that is, memorable and simple). This is the same process you went through for identifying your own.

Find the one that is the best, and work to counter that specific story. Try to get opposing counsel to adopt the story that is the lowest on the combination of the three factors. Most likely they will pick the story that they feel is most on their side, even if that is not believable or does not fit the facts very well.

If opposing counsel stubbornly pushes a story that is not believable or does not fit the facts, don't get frustrated that you are unable to get them to admit that their case is weak. This is exactly what you want!

Opposing counsel will rarely openly admit that they might lose and they will always come up with some reasoning justifying the merits of their case, no matter how weak or silly it sounds. Instead of getting frustrated or angry that they are stretching credulity, you should thank them (figuratively) and smile (literally). When things don't go their way and they lose motion after motion or depositions turn out to be disasters for them and they say to you "I can't believe this judge" or "your dirty deposition tactics won't win this case for you," simply shrug.

Once you deduce the story that they are likely going to tell, you need to know how they're going to tell it – what documents and witnesses they're using to tell the story. You also need to know how you're telling your story and which documents and witnesses that are in their possession that you want to use to help tell your story. You cannot limit your discovery to only the story that they are likely going to tell because they might change their story at any time.

But focus on the areas that fit all of the stories, and then those that fit their best stories, and last the ones that fit their weakest stories.

Discovery Guidelines

Start discovery immediately.

Focus your written discovery; do not use a shotgun approach (unless it is for strategic reasons, such as the "Attrition" strategy that I discuss in Part IV).

Use interrogatories to get their story and theory, use document demands to get their potential exhibits, and use requests for admission to pin them down to one story. You can also use requests for admission to create the possibility of recovering attorney's fees where it might not otherwise exist: California, for example, allows "cost of proof" sanctions in some instances if a party unreasonably denies a request for admission and it is proven at trial they should have admitted to the request instead.

All three forms of discovery will reveal their witnesses.

Probably the most common approach to discovery is to embark on a fishing expedition and seek everything under the sun. Too many lawyers fight over what they are "entitled to receive," end up spending hundreds of hours in discovery disputes and motions, and then all of this evidence sits and collects dust until a month before trial.

But you do not need to propound hundreds of interrogatories asking about each and every contention! That approach will get you hundreds of pages of copy/pasted responses, which will make more work for you to review. This ends up wasting time and money.

Worse, it gives you far too much useless information that you have to weed through and leaves you unable to crystalize your case.

It makes any motion to compel burdensome and unfocused, and the opposing counsel will be justified in requesting multiple extensions of time to respond.

Instead, focus your discovery so that it is easy and very little work for you to compel. You will get better information and you will get it quickly. If you have to compel, the papers will be concise and the judge will be more likely to go your way, and even grant discovery sanctions.

Many lawyers constantly wonder why they can't get discovery sanctions even when they win a motion to compel. The reason is that the discovery requests appear unfocused and unnecessary even to the judge!

From the start of a case, you should know what evidence exists (although you might not know what it says) and what you need in order to present your case at trial. This is true in 99% of cases.

If, at the beginning of the case you do not know what evidence exists, how to get it, and what you will need to present your case at trial, then chances are you have not adequately developed your preliminary theory, story, and theme.

Purposely pick your strategies based on the situation. Maintain flexibility in evolving and changing strategies and tactics as the case evolves.

Remember the adage by the wise sage Tyson: "Everyone has a plan until they get punched in the mouth."

> **TIP**
>
> Attorneys will often serve a motion or opposition on the last possible day in order to give their opponents the least amount of time to research and prepare a responsive brief.
>
> This is a poor tactic.
>
> If there is a problem with the filing or service, you will not have time to correct it. Obviously, if you need the time in order to prepare the brief, then you should take the time. But if you are done early, go ahead and serve and file it early.
>
> You are not gaining a tangible advantage by waiting, and instead are taking unnecessary risk. Good lawyers will prepare good work product even with little time, and bad lawyers will not prepare good work product even with abundant time.

•
SKILLS YOU CAN'T OUTSOURCE TO YOUR CLIENT
•

You might have the best, most helpful client on Earth, and you still shouldn't make any assumptions about their skills, understanding, or ability to get you the information you need. Clients typically don't have legal training, and they never have access to your thoughts. They filter every explanation you provide and question you ask through their own ideas about what a lawyer needs to know, what you already know, what is relevant to the case, and what puts them in the best light.

Here are some essential responsibilities that belong to you, the lawyer, and should never be outsourced onto your client.

ORGANIZATION

Lawyers must be organized. You must have ready access to every detail of evidence, and every aspect of the law. It is impossible to have everything memorized, and a strong system of organization solves this problem.

It is certainly helpful if your client is organized, but they may not be. And, even the most organized client has a system that is tailored to their situation, and might not be ideal for quickly retrieving and analyzing the information you need. So, be specific about what you need from your client, ask follow up questions to make sure your client isn't missing information that is stored somewhere else, and organize what you receive in the way that is best for your case. Don't assume your client has easy access to information.

FOLLOW-UP

You can write as many "CYA" letters as you want, and that might protect you from a lawsuit if something goes wrong; but you should not realistically expect your client to make note of, or act on, what you advise in those letters. It is your job to follow up on important information, even if you told your client to contact you with any questions.

Assume your client files your letters away after a quick glance. If something is important, follow up until you are satisfied that they actually understood and absorbed what you were trying to communicate.

Planning

It may seem as if a client has sufficient information when they sign your retainer agreement. Between the agreement and your initial client interview, you thoroughly explained that litigation is a time consuming, expensive, and often stressful undertaking that will require certain things from them over the next weeks, months, and maybe years. They have all the information they need to plan their budget and time accordingly.

Yet, too often friction starts between lawyer and client within the first six months of representation because the client did not plan for the inevitable complications that arise from a lawsuit.

Clients should not be expected to fully understand what happens during a lawsuit. Most people have little experience with the legal system, and a lot of misperceptions. It is your job to plan out the case, explain the plan and anything that might happen to disrupt that plan, and revisit the explanation regularly to make sure the client is still on board.

The better you become at thinking through possible scenarios and contingencies, the better your cases will proceed.

Investigation

The job of investigation – both the direct investigation of the case and the related investigation needed to determine how the case could impact the rest of your client's life – falls on the lawyer, not the client.

Your client may not know what information you need or where to get it, and may be making assumptions about what is relevant and what isn't, especially when it comes to embarrassing or problematic information and evidence.

Your client may not realize that what you do in litigation could have real life consequences. Those consequences might affect your client's reputation, business, or family. There may be tax or other financial consequences that the client should – but doesn't know enough to – discuss with a CPA or other financial professional. Or, the consequences might be related to other claims or litigation, since your client could admit something in your case that affects other claims.

Tailor your investigation not only to the facts that are directly relevant to the case, but also to different aspects that may affect your client's decision making. This can be difficult and intrusive, so you must approach this aspect of your investigation with care.

OBJECTIVE EVALUATION

Clients have a lot invested in their litigation, both financially and emotionally. They cannot be expected to see both sides or internalize the strengths and weaknesses of their cases. Yet, too many lawyers stop being objective as soon as they are retained, and their clients miss out on that crucial reality check.

Make sure that you have an unbiased and objective understanding of your case, so you can craft the best possible strategies and arguments and advise your client based on reality, and not wishful thinking.

IN SUMMARY

The human brain is a marvel. It is also extremely lazy and relies on pattern recognition and assumptions to save time and energy.

No matter how good your work ethic, you cannot change your brain's tendency to find shortcuts in thinking.

As a lawyer, you must accept this and develop ways to identify the assumptions that your brain is forcing onto you. Often, this means that you will make assumptions about your clients' abilities that you should not be making. Instead, make sure that you are not relying on your clients, but instead develop the following skills for yourself:

- Organization.

- Follow-up.

- Planning.

- Investigation.

- Objective evaluation.

MICRO-SKILLS BEYOND THE BASICS

Successfully litigating a case is not a matter of going through the motions (literally or figuratively). It requires applying the right skills at the right time. Sometimes you want to persuade in writing, sometimes on the phone or in person. Other times the best approach may not be to persuade; rather, it may be to listen and empathize.

Whatever your goal in the moment, it is important to understand that there are distinct categories of skillsets. To excel at litigation, you need to know what these skills are, work to improve at all of them, and learn when to apply each.

In this chapter, I identify some of these skillsets and provide an overview on how to improve them. In the Further Reading section at the end of this book, I identify specific books that will help you drill down and perfect specific skills.

For the best return on the investment of your time, you should try to identify one or two areas of personal weakness and focus on improving those first. For instance, you might be a technically excellent writer but unpersuasive because of tone or structural problems. You may have mastered written persuasion but find that you come across very differently in a spoken presentation. Or you might be right at home in trial but uncomfortable in the more cooperative aspects of your job, like counseling clients or participating in settlement discussions.

Be honest with yourself: we all have room for improvement!

The four categories of skills covered in this chapter are:

- Written.
- Spoken advocacy.
- Analytical skills.
- Interpersonal/emotional skills.

WRITTEN SKILLS

In considering written skills, I am referring primarily to briefs and pleadings. These may be a complaint, motion, pre-trial brief, etc.

Although the skills referred here are not directly referring to forms of communication such as letters or emails, they will carry over to those non-argumentative forms of writing.

I have observed that lawyers are often weak in two fundamental areas of their writing:

- Persuasion.
- Tone.

Persuasion

Writing persuasively requires a subtle understanding of how being persuasive differs from being confident and aggressive.

A motion, or other brief, written without a sense of objectivity – using words like "clearly," and "obviously," or hiding the ball on weaknesses – may be confident and aggressive... but it isn't persuasive. And it creates the perfect opportunity for your opponent to discredit you by exposing whatever weak point you tried to hide or whatever disputed point you tried to make certain.

> **TIP**
>
> Neither your opponent nor your judge is stupid. When you completely ignore, or gloss over, your weak points, you are significantly hurting your side. Worse, if you feel you cannot prove your point except by hiding your weaknesses, then it means you have not fully developed your argument.

Persuasive writing begins with the first words below the caption. Do not start with throat clearing.

There is no purpose to using anachronistic phrases such as "Comes now Plaintiff before this honorable court and complains of Defendant as follows," or "in response to Defendant's demurrer, Plaintiff hereby submits, for consideration by this court, the following opposition."

I challenge you to find a Rule of Court or Code of Procedure that requires this verbiage, and it immediately weakens your brief. Instead, start with a heading (e.g., "Introduction"), and begin immediately: "This case arises from Defendant's breach of contract," or "Defendant's demurrer should be overruled because..."

SKIPPING THE LEARNING CURVE

Aside from getting right to the point, you should also focus on getting your winning argument across *within the first page* of your document. This is when your judge's attention and information absorption is at its highest. This is when you can make your greatest impact. Do not waste this valuable real estate it with unnecessary fluff. For instance, do not begin with a recitation of procedural history or law. Focus on answering one and only one question: why do I win? If you are submitting an opposition document, concede valid points in your introduction and explain why it doesn't matter in a sentence or two.

If you cannot explain why your opponent is wrong in a few sentences, then you will not be able to explain it in a few pages. Ask yourself: are they using the wrong rule? Are they making assumptions? Does the evidence not support their conclusion? Focus on the logic of the argument instead of the emotion or distractions and you will be more persuasive.

Likewise, your "Conclusion" section should not be wasted. Do not ever end on a single sentence along the lines of "Wherefore, Defendant's demurrer must be sustained." Instead, summarize, in no more than two short paragraphs, your entire argument before getting to the requested relief.

Like the introduction and conclusion, the main body of your brief should focus on what matters. Summarize the Rule and its elements (without misstating it). Focus on the facts and the application of the facts to the law.

> **TIP**
>
> It might seem obvious, but the most important part of your brief is the application of the facts to the law. Despite the seemingly obvious nature of this statement, it is unfortunately common to see more words spent summarizing the law and procedure.
>
> If you are spending more words on law or procedural summaries than you are on the facts, evidence, and application of the law, then you are losing.

To help you with the above guidelines, try these three techniques that will instantly increase your written persuasiveness:

Organization and planning

From the first word you put on a page, your organization and planning is crucial.

- **Begin your Reply brief with your Moving brief:** If you represent the moving party to a motion, keep a separate document, *as you draft your moving brief*, titled "Reply Notes" to keep ideas for your Reply. You should be able to know what their opposition argument is going to be, and you should be able to mold your moving brief in a way that leaves your Reply stronger.

- **Prevent surprise arguments in your Opponent's Reply:** If you represent the Opposing Party, watch out for arguments that the moving party might be trying to "save for Reply." They will often drop a hint of this by putting a case in a citation, or using a stray word or sentence that seems a little out of place. That way they have a plausible argument that they're not raising the point for the first time in Reply (although they're not supposed to do that, a lot of lawyers do it anyway since there's no undoing the damage). With a careful reading and a good understanding of the arguments, you should be able to know what these possible points will be. You should then pre-emptively address them in your Opposition brief.

- **Don't throw in the kitchen sink:** You don't need to argue every single argument that you have thought about. However, you do need to raise any argument that you want to preserve for appeal, and dropping an argument in a footnote might not be enough. Nonetheless, focus on those arguments that rise above a certain strength threshold. That threshold might change depending on the importance of the motion. Any weak arguments that go below that threshold that you want to preserve for appeal should be minimized in focus so you have done enough to raise them, but you haven't distracted from your winning arguments.

Properly incorporate cases

- **Understand the purpose of a case:** A case is useful for two purposes. The first is to provide the Rule, the second is to provide facts that will be used for analogy or context. Some cases provide only one use, some provide both, and some provide a hybrid. Figure out why you are using a case, and then incorporate it appropriately depending on whether it states the rule or will be compared for facts.

- **If the Rule is straightforward, don't overexplain:** If a case is included for the Rule only, then you don't need to describe the fact pattern. It is sufficient to say, for instance, "A party may plead alternative theories" and then provide a citation without giving an example. If the Rule is central to the argument and the main thrust of the opposition, then use string citations to show that the Rule is well-established. Often, the case facts are irrelevant. If they are irrelevant, don't waste space with them.

- **If the Rule is unsettled or might not apply, then use the case facts to explain why it applies:** If the Rule is only applicable in certain situations, then you need to explain the case facts as well in order to demonstrate when the Rule applies. But you may do so briefly. If this is the situation, address it even though it requires you to admit that there are situations where the Rule might not apply.

- **Use the case facts if you need to draw comparisons, whether the Rule is certain or not:** If you want to show that other courts have ruled a certain way *given similar facts*, then you need to spell out the facts and draw comparisons. This is almost never necessary. Almost every case can be distinguished in some way. It is not helpful to a judge to know how a case that was similar, but with some distinguishing facts, came out. An example of when a comparison of the facts is useful would be in an Intentional Infliction of Emotional Distress case. To prove IIED, a plaintiff needs to show "extreme and outrageous" behavior. So a comparison to cases showing "this behavior was extreme and outrageous; this behavior was not; ours is more like this behavior" is necessary in some situations. But generally, the most useful information to explain is: (1) the Rule, (2) whether it is set in stone or rarely applied, and (3) in what situations it does not apply.

Properly incorporate the evidence

Remember that the facts and evidence in your specific case are more important than the facts in any other case you cite. Use the supporting cases to establish the Rule that applies, and then focus on applying that Rule to your case. This is where the bulk of your writing should focus, and it should be in-depth. Ask two questions in making your argument:

- Which of my facts are well-established?

- Which of my facts can be fairly disputed?

Then explain why your facts fit the Rule in an honest manner. If facts are unsettled, address them head-on in your brief, admitting that the facts are disputed but that you still win either because: (1) it does not matter how those facts turn out, or (2) your presentation of the facts is more likely to be the truth.

Tone

Tone goes hand-in-hand with persuasion. A persuasive argument can lose its impact if your tone is off, and otherwise valid points lose credibility. An argument that otherwise seems weaker will be more persuasive if your tone is appealing, especially if your counterpart's tone is not.

Strive for a balanced tone.

Don't attack the other side or get overly creative with language. Leave the adverbs out. When you claim that something is "obviously" some way, you are telling a judge that it is not that way.

Remain professional. Don't get overly casual or cutesy; avoid clichés or casual metaphors like "that dog won't hunt." Always remind yourself not to waste words.

Have humility and a conversational approach. Re-write anything that is a personal attack or is designed to satisfy that little voice inside your heart that wants to say "Ha! That was a good shot at opposing counsel!"

If the judge reads your papers and can envision you standing before him rolling your eyes or shaking your head, then your tone is off.

> **EXERCISE**
>
> - Review a past motion that you lost but you feel you should have won.
>
> - Did the judge misunderstand the law or the facts or the application of the facts to the law?
>
> - Compare the amount of space spent writing about the law (cases, statutes, rules, etc.) to that spent discussing the facts.
>
> - Did you unnecessarily go into detail explaining the Rule or the facts from a case?

Spoken Advocacy

When trying to figure out how to "argue," it is easy to revert back to the old adage that "when the facts are on your side, pound the facts; when the law is on your side, pound the law; when neither the facts nor the law are on your side, pound the table."

Sometimes it seems like lawyers are supposed to pound the table anyway, just for fun.

In order to make a very persuasive argument, we have to do something counter-intuitive: we have to be, or at least seem, objective. The decision maker should view us as the voice of reason, just explaining how things are; not the hired gun spinning the facts to whatever conclusion helps our client.

Beyond Basic Skills

Credibility is key: this means calmly addressing the opposing viewpoint so it is clear that you understand and have considered it, conceding good points raised by opposing counsel, and carefully monitoring your tone for contempt and sarcasm.

Also, don't be afraid of silence. There is no rule saying that the lawyer with the most words wins. In fact, usually the lawyer doing the talking is losing. Take time to think before you answer a question, pause to let an important point sink in, and, most importantly, if you are winning, don't talk and screw it up!

TIP

One of the first cases I ever had was representing a plaintiff with a very weak case. I informed my client before even filing that opposing counsel will likely file a demurrer and will likely win. Sure enough, opposing counsel filed a demurrer, and the tentative ruling was to sustain the demurrer *without* leave to amend.

At the hearing, the judge asked opposing counsel if he had anything to add to his argument. Opposing counsel then spent *ten minutes* explaining, ironically, that the most important lesson he had learned in his decades of practice was to be quiet when the tentative was in your favor.

Without me having to say a word, the judge changed his tentative and gave me leave to amend.

Lesson: don't do that! Judges are busy and don't have time for your braggadocio. In their courtroom they don't want to hear about your experience or accomplishments (at a social setting they might not mind).

If public speaking isn't a natural skill for you, don't worry. There are many resources that can help. There are classes and groups that can provide practice opportunities, and many books and videos to help you learn breath control and other speaking techniques. Oratory skills are helpful, but not the deciding factor. It is far more important to be credible than an eloquent speaker.

ANALYTICAL SKILLS

Many lawyers believe that law school taught them "to think like a lawyer," and that may be true. But it is a sentence worth unpacking. What kind of "thinking" must a lawyer master in order to excel?

There are only a few key concepts to know about legal argument. If you differentiate these in your mind, you will be able to focus your arguments.

The IRAC Framework

As a foundation, it is helpful to review the "IRAC" formula from law school and how it applies in actual practice:

- **Issue:** This sets the foundation for the argument. For instance, is the question whether or not plaintiff has standing or whether or not the proper cause of action is pled? This is important, because if you believe the issue in a demurrer is whether or not the evidence will support the plaintiff's case, then you will lose because that is not the proper focus of that type of motion. You must be able to properly identify, explain, and prioritize the issues of a legal question in order to frame the argument.

- **Rule/Law:** This can come from statutes, caselaw, or elsewhere depending on the issue. You must be able to identify the proper rule or rules that apply to the issue. If you use the wrong rule for consideration of the relevant issue, then you will lose.

- **Facts:** These are the specific circumstances of your case that are supported by evidence. There is a bit of a recursive process because the issue gets defined by the facts and the law. You must be able to differentiate between "alleged" facts and "supported" facts. All facts should be viewed as "alleged" until you examine the evidence. And the evidence can strongly or weakly prove or disprove a fact.

    You should not try to squeeze evidence into proving facts that you hope to be true. Rather, you should describe the facts that the evidence supports and use logic to prove your points. Lawyers often refer to "good" or "bad" facts, and "good" or "bad" evidence. But there are not "good" or "bad" facts and evidence. There are just facts and evidence. Some of them tell a more believable story than others, and that will naturally lead to some stories favoring or disfavoring your desired outcome.

    But don't look at the facts and evidence and think of it as "good" or "bad." Doing so will cause you to try to spin a story and be less believable. Instead, just accept the facts and see all of the stories that could exist. Then focus on the one that most suits your case and the law. Tell it as it is, not how you wish it to be.

- **Conclusion:** This is a statement of what should happen based on the issue, law, and facts. This is the logical outcome of your analysis.

If you keep those items as distinct concepts in your mind, and apply certain analytical skills, your arguments will be clearer and more persuasive.

> **TIP**
>
> The IRAC framework is not just a law-school relic. I see lawyers constantly filing motions that are pre-destined to lose because they are not focused on the right aspects.
>
> Using the IRAC framework will help you on a macro level by guiding the development of your theory, and also on a micro level, in arguing individual motions.
>
> Don't feel silly outlining your arguments using such a "basic" tool. Judges process arguments using it, either consciously or subconsciously.

Aside from the IRAC framework, there are four analytical skills that will elevate your practice:

- Objectivity.
- Logic.
- Curiosity.
- Patience.

Working to develop all four separately, and knowing how they interact, is crucial to developing your analytical skills.

Objectivity

The first analytical skill that will elevate your practice is objectivity, an especially difficult skill because the nature of law practice encourages us to view cases from just one side.

We must walk a fine line, taking on the role of advocate for our client without losing sight of the broader view; while we must act like an advocate, we must also be able to think like a judge. Examining and understanding opposing arguments and theories is crucial to developing the strongest possible case. Remember that your opponent often believes his or her story as deeply as you do yours.

Logic

The second analytical skill is an understanding of logic. Basic legal argument is structured as a form of deductive reasoning called a "syllogism."

In its most basic form, a syllogism follows a specific formula to reach a conclusion:

- All X are Y (the "Major Premise")

- Z is X (the "Minor Premise")

- Therefore, Z is Y (the "Conclusion")

In legal argument, the law (commonly called the "rule") is the "Major Premise" and the application of facts to the law is the "Minor Premise."

SKIPPING THE LEARNING CURVE

You have to understand the structure of logic in order to make persuasive argument. Otherwise, you are shooting in the dark.

For instance, in a breach of contract case, you may be making the following argument:

- To be an enforceable contract (X), there must be consideration (Y).

- The contract between John and Jane (Z) did not have consideration (Y).

- Therefore, the contract between John and Jane (Z) is not an enforceable contract (X).

Notice that although this example follows the basic structure of a syllogism, it is presented slightly differently than the basic formula: "to be X, there must be Y; Z does *not* have Y; thus, Z is not X."

There are many ways to approach argument, and I encourage you to learn more about the topic. But for now, understanding the concept of a syllogism and how it fits into legal argument is a great start.

When preparing your argument, ask the following questions:

- Is your opponent using the wrong rule (Major Premise)?

- Is your opponent misstating the rule or the facts (*i.e.,* is the Major or Minor Premise incorrect)? This is slightly different than using the wrong rule in that here they are straying from the rule or facts and creating something that is not true or not supported. In contract, in using the wrong rule, they may be making an otherwise true or supported statement, but it is irrelevant to the situation.

- Is your opponent drawing an incorrect conclusion (*e.g.,* because the Major Premise is not the one to use for this issue or the Minor Premise is not supported by the evidence)?

For instance, if your opponent argued "there is an enforceable contract because John ran a red light," the implicit rule (*i.e.* the "Major Premise") is that "running a red light creates an enforceable contract." This is obviously an entirely wrong rule to use in a breach of contract case. And so, even though it might be true that John ran a red light, your argument should be focused on proving that it is the *wrong rule*.

Many lawyers might instinctually argue – in addition to any other points – that John did not run the red light. But you should not waste time on whether or not John ran a red light (assuming there is no cause of action for negligence based on running a red light). Depending on the context, you can object to the fact as irrelevant, waive it off with a brief statement such as "whether or not John ran the red light, there is no enforceable contract here because…," or simply ignore altogether (there is a difference between ignoring weak arguments, which you should not do, and ignoring frivolous arguments, which you may choose to do).

On the other hand, if your opponent argued "there is an enforceable contract even though there was no consideration," then they must be able to support the rule that "not all contracts require consideration," and the focus of your argument will be different.

Once you understand the structure of a syllogism, then the weaknesses in your opponents' arguments will jump out at you. Everything you do – your writing, oral argument, and even presentations to a judge or jury – will be significantly more focused and persuasive. This will also help you create a strong story and undermine opposing stories.

> **TIP**
>
> This is where the work outlining your arguments using the IRAC framework really pays off!
>
> If you understand how a logical syllogism works, then you will be able to identify whether your opponent is addressing the wrong issue, using the wrong rule (or misstating it), misapplying the evidence to the facts or the facts to the law, or otherwise drawing the wrong conclusion. You will also be able to identify and address the flaws in your own arguments.

Curiosity

The third analytical skill is to keep an open mind and remain curious. You need to actively seek out and incorporate things outside of your theory. Don't assume that you understand things completely, and don't assume your client has told you everything, or even the truth.

As humans, we have an amazing ability to rewrite history. Your clients may tell you what they honestly believe to be true, and the evidence may still strongly disagree with your clients' perception of events. Or your clients may tell you what they think defines their case, and that may not be the most important issue at all. You will also be surprised at the amount of useful information you can learn from the other side by being curious.

Patience

The fourth analytical skill is to take your time. Spend a few extra minutes listening to your client, even after you think you have all the information you need. Let your mind wander over your case during passive time – in the car, the shower, while you cook dinner – because you will make different connections than you will at your desk.

Start projects early, so you'll have some of that crucial passive time before your deadline. Do a little extra research, read that important case slower, and give everything you write one extra review. If you are rushed, you will always miss things.

EXERCISE

During your free time, review the most recent brief that you filed in court. Chances are you will find a typo, grammar error, or some other change that you wish you could correct.

Interpersonal/Emotional Skills

We are all happier when we take care of ourselves emotionally. And, for people who work in the world of conflict, the importance of developing strong interpersonal skills and emotional intelligence can't be overstated.

We deal with difficult clients, colleagues, and opposing counsel, as well as tight deadlines. Stress is part of the job description for many of us. Learning to recognize and manage our reactions to these inevitable pressures can make the difference between enjoying a challenging career and slogging miserably to the end of each workday.

Interpersonal and emotional intelligence skills are independent, although closely related.

Interpersonal skills that most lawyers need to improve are:

- **Empathy:** If you can understand how a situation looks from someone else's perspective, you can probably communicate effectively with that person. But most of us fall into the trap, at least sometimes, of assuming we see the world exactly the way it is. Actually, there are as many perspectives as there are people, and it is always worth asking yourself how the world looks and feels to other people. Get curious about other people's experiences and you will quickly learn to connect with them.

- **Listening skills:** Listening is more than just hearing the words that come out of someone else's mouth. And yet most of us can improve our listening just by committing to this first, basic step. Start with an intention to be quiet while other people talk. Just giving others the space to express themselves without interruption will make you a next-level listener. Then, develop a listening mindset where you go into every interaction with a desire to understand the other person. That means asking questions to help the other person expand and clarify their message, demonstrating understanding and being open to correction, and cultivating an attitude of non-judgmental curiosity while listening. You might be surprised by how many arguments can be avoided this way.

- **Negotiation and problem-solving skills:** By negotiation and problem solving, I don't just mean getting the best deal you can. I mean the ability to work with another person or a group of people to generate solutions to a problem in a way that protects your client's interests without shutting down discussion, limiting options, or burning bridges. Negotiation is much more complex than merely setting an anchor number and inching towards the middle.

TRUE STORY

In a real estate arbitration where we represented the Petitioner, we negotiated a settlement that just needed a signed agreement to complete the matter. Crucial to negotiating the settlement was that the Respondent knew that he could bring a case for indemnity against his real estate broker to attempt to recoup some of the settlement money.

When I reviewed the draft settlement agreement put together by opposing counsel, I noticed that it would potentially release his client's claims against the broker. Obviously, this was not a direct concern for me or my client. Nonetheless, after discussing with my client, I called opposing counsel and said "Hi Bob, in looking over this agreement, I wonder how this language might affect your client if he ever brought a case against the broker. Take a look and let me know if you want to make any edits or if you're ok with it."

A few days later, the lawyer called me "a gentleman and a scholar" and sent over a revised agreement. I thanked him and also negotiated slightly better terms for my client, which he was happy to provide.

Even though his error was not my problem, correcting it resulted in an even better outcome for my client. Equally as important, if the broker ended up asserting the settlement agreement as part of his defense in a later lawsuit, that could – theoretically – lead to my client being dragged into the dispute or fighting over the validity of the agreement.

Emotional intelligence is an entire discipline that can be studied. But here are some immediate skills that will help you professionally and personally:

- **Self-control:** Self-control doesn't sound like much fun, does it? It is essential, though, if you want to be in charge of your own life. By self-control I don't mean shutting off your feelings or denying yourself pleasure. I mean learning to respond instead of react, so that you are in charge of how you interact with people and situations. Work to recognize the triggers that tend to make you react in unhelpful ways, and learn to pause. Mindfulness training can be helpful here.

- **Emotional expression:** The flip side of good self-control is constructive emotional expression. You won't be happy or healthy if you get really good at controlling yourself, but you have no idea how to explain how you feel. Work to develop the self-knowledge to see and understand your feelings, the language to share them honestly, respectfully, and as kindly as possible with others, and the courage to be vulnerable when you need to be.

- **Motivation:** Everything you do is the result of motivation, but many of us have no idea how we are motivated. Figure out what makes you excited to move forward, and what makes you feel stuck or paralyzed. This is an important key not just to productivity, but also to happiness.

IN SUMMARY

As a lawyer, you should constantly look to improve a number of skills:

- **Written**
    - *Persuasion*
        - Organization and planning
        - Properly incorporating cases
        - Properly incorporating evidence
    - *Tone*

- **Spoken**

- **Analytic**
    - *IRAC framework*
    - *Logic/syllogism*
    - *Curiosity*
    - *Patience*

- **Interpersonal/Emotional**
    - *Empathy*
    - *Listening*
    - *Negotiation and problem-solving*
    - *Self-control*
    - *Emotional expression*
    - *Motivation*

PART III

SETTLEMENT LEVERAGE POINTS AND THE KEYSTONE OF THE CASE

The Tale of the Persuasive Coach

"A business coach named John was giving one of his famous talks on the power of persuasion to a packed lecture hall.

A jealous rival shouted out 'your techniques are bupkis! People only do what you say because you have a famous name, and that's only from marketing! I bet you can't persuade me of anything!'

The lecture hall went silent, but John only smiled and responded: 'Ok. I will take you up on your challenge. Why don't you come up to the front here and I will see what I can do?'

The jealous rival jumped at the opportunity to embarrass John. He proudly marched to the front, chest puffed up.

As he approached, John said 'Great, come stand to my left over here and we can get started.'

The rival did that.

'Actually,' John said, 'the light is better on my right. Why don't you stand on this side?'

The rival went to the other side.

John spread his arms wide to the audience and announced 'the power of persuasion!'

The audience erupted in applause, and the rival slunk back to his seat."

> *"Therefore the skillful leader subdues the enemy's troops without any fighting; he captures their cities without laying siege to them; he overthrows their kingdom without lengthy operations in the field."*
>
> *— Sun Tzu*

We cannot force people to do what we want. For instance, if someone refuses to pay money that they owe, we cannot go into their bank account and take the money. But the government can!

That is the purpose of a lawsuit. At its most basic, a lawsuit is a request you make to the government, asking it to impose a consequence. By contrast, a settlement is the result of convincing someone to act voluntarily.

Often, cases take unexpected paths to settlement. You might have a solid case that seems like it should settle early, but the parties fight until the day before trial. Or you might have a case that seems destined for a jury, but opposing counsel suddenly becomes eager to settle. It can be unpredictable.

Settlement decisions are not always based on the raw merits of the case. Plaintiffs and defendants do not always make a clear, mathematical, cost/benefit decision when they decide whether to settle or move forward in court.

Settlement Leverage Points and the Keystone of the Case

If you ask most lawyers to identify the goal of a case, they will say:

- The plaintiff wants to get as much money as possible.

- The defendant wants to pay as little money as possible.

This is only a surface explanation of complex human decision-making.

To understand settlement motivations, we need to start with a client's perspective. If you have clients who are sophisticated litigators, they probably go into lawsuits with more realistic expectations. But for clients who spend very little time in court, assessing risk in a lawsuit is difficult.

Generally, the clients/parties in a case see three, and only three, possible results:

1. **They lose.** The plaintiff defines this as a court or jury "going against them." They typically view the consequence as resulting in them being out of pocket their own legal fees and costs (or if it's a contingency case, then they're out nothing). They don't imagine a worse outcome than losing their own legal fees, even if there is a risk that they will have to pay the other side's costs and fees and they have verbally acknowledged this. In their hearts, they don't believe a loss of any sort can happen outside a complete travesty of justice.

2. **They are made whole.** To the plaintiff, this means that they both win some amount of money AND get back their legal fees and costs. They may acknowledge the possibility of "winning" and not actually being made whole, either due to a small judgment or the high cost of the litigation, but they don't really believe that this is the most likely possibility. To a defendant, being whole at the end of the lawsuit means they are vindicated *and* the plaintiff pays their legal fees and costs.

3. **Jackpot!** This is the outcome that most parties, deep down, believe is the likely result. Even sophisticated individuals and businesses (which are really a collection of individuals) believe that they will have a jackpot. The definition of "jackpot" varies from person to person; nonetheless, whether a party is a plaintiff or defendant, most believe they will come out of the lawsuit *in a better position* than they went into it. Plaintiffs have visions of a jury awarding one of those lottery wins you read about sometimes. Defendants often believe in the merits of a strategically filed cross-complaint, and don't truly understand that there isn't a realistic possibility of an award in their favor.

Since these are the three possible outcomes clients see, and their emotional understanding of the possibility of losing tends to be shaky, the only outcomes they are emotionally prepared to discuss are (2) (being made whole) and (3) (jackpot).

Settlement Leverage Points and the Keystone of the Case

If a jackpot is possible in their minds, and a loss is almost impossible, that means gambling on the lawsuit feels worth it. To a plaintiff, logic dictates that they file the lawsuit and litigate it; to a defendant, it means fight instead of settle.

To the extent they may accept that a complete jackpot is not necessarily the most likely outcome, they view the range of outcomes as a sliding scale between (2) and (3). They understand that they might not have a complete "jackpot," but can't imagine coming out of the lawsuit worse than they went into it.

On the other hand, the lawyer's realistic range is a worst-case scenario of negative money (since their client might have to pay the other side's attorney's fees, costs, or both), to a best-case outcome of being made *less than whole* (since the client will have to pay legal fees and costs in some form, either up front or as a percentage of the recovery).

Being made truly whole, or hitting a jackpot are unlikely, but hoped for, results – a smart lawyer wouldn't advise a client to plan for that level of success. Viewed on the scale above, that means that the lawyer views the range of outcomes at less than (2) and, in the worst case, some negative number that is not on the client's scale.

In other words, parties to lawsuits don't believe the middle ground between a loss and (2) is possible, and lawyers take this middle ground for granted, since that's what they see all the time. Based on these perceived outcomes, clients and lawyers both try to calculate whether and when they should settle a case.

The rough math that both clients and lawyers do, whether or not they realize it, is "what are the odds of winning" multiplied by "what is the best/worst case at trial." They then compare the fees and costs to get there and see how a settlement compares.

In theory, this number should be roughly the same for the plaintiff and defendant. Most people explain a failure to reach agreement on that number as a difference in opinion about the chance of winning. But it goes beyond that.

Law is not a simple math problem, and the discrepancies between a party's view of possible outcomes and their lawyer's view of possible outcomes can lead to bad settlement decisions. People are not calculators, and we have all seen many cases where the plaintiff spends more money in litigation expenses than he could possibly win, or where the defendant could have settled a case earlier for a fraction of what he ends up spending. So, this simple cost benefit-analysis must not be so simple, after all.

These "illogical" results can come from optimism, overconfidence, or a mistake in evaluating the case. Sometimes, the attorney is at fault. Sometimes the client is at fault. Sometimes, no one is at fault – there are a lot of variables in a litigated case, and even the best predictors can't foresee everything. But if you want to have the best chance of settling your case favorably, you need a deeper understanding of what drives plaintiffs, defendants, and their attorneys as they make settlement decisions.

Settlement Leverage Points and the Keystone of the Case

A lawsuit is actually never about the money, and money is not the engine of litigation that drives the parties. Money is the *oil* that allows the engine of litigation to turn. And money is the *destination* because it is the only option the legal system can provide (setting aside injunctions, which are rare and only allowed when money truly won't do).

The true engine of a lawsuit is *emotion*: anger, fear, ego, and every other emotion people can feel. Even when the emotion is greed, the lawsuit is about the greed and not the money. Discovering and staying in touch with each sides' true goal – your client's as well – is essential.

Cases settle when the settlement satisfies the goals and emotions of both sides. Those goals can shift – a plaintiff might start a case with the goal of driving the defendant out of business, but after two years of fighting, he might have a new goal of staying in business himself. Or maybe a defendant, early in a case, has the goal of making money on his cross-complaint, but after a few rounds of discovery and a bad deposition, he decides he just wants to get out without paying much.

Often, there are things driving your case that don't seem relevant to you, as the attorney, but have a huge effect on negotiations. If you can do the detective work necessary to learn what these hidden motivators are, you will be better able to craft a satisfying settlement.

This chapter explains how to identify the underlying factors of a lawsuit and the true goals of the parties, as well as the outside forces that influence decision-making, how these factors and goals fit into the "win" calculus, and how to use all of this information to help your clients.

SKIPPING THE LEARNING CURVE

TIP

A client with little litigation experience is likely to believe he will receive justice quickly once he does his part by hiring you and filing that first paper. Six months down the road, with substantial legal bills and seemingly little progress to show for it, the same client is likely to have regrets, and those regrets can lead to bad settlement decisions. Managing your clients' expectations from the start increases the chance that your client will pursue a sound litigation strategy.

When you hear any of the following statements, it is time to explore your client's assumptions and expectations:

- "They will settle as soon as they see this smoking gun document!" (When the document is already known to the other side or, in your opinion, doesn't seem significant enough to end the case).

- "The judge will go my way as soon as you explain it to her - when is your next hearing?" (When you are far from trial and the judge won't be making a substantive decision for many months).

- "They have to pay me whatever I want because they can't risk the bad press!" (When you know the press won't be so bad, the client has already blabbed the story all over town, or you think the defendant has a strong stomach for bad press.)

- "They will pay me as soon as they understand what a bad thing they did!" (This one is always a red flag.)

Settlement Leverage Points and the Keystone of the Case

•
GOAL VALUE
•

An ongoing endeavor in any representation must be to figure out the true goal of your client. It is rare that your client will explain their true goal. Sometimes they will think that you won't take the case or you won't try hard if they explain their true goal. Other times, they won't even understand what they really want.

You must ask questions about the surrounding circumstances and draw your own conclusions.

These are the primary driving forces beyond the raw merits of the case:

Long term strategy vs. this case: A client might justify a strategy that doesn't make mathematical sense if there are long term considerations. For instance, a large company might be willing to pay their attorneys to defend employment cases instead of settling early in order to dissuade lawyers from taking contingency cases against them.

This strategy can work in the long run… although it is worth exploring this motivation, as clients sometimes imagine a "slippery slope" where there really isn't much risk that settlement will lead to more litigation.

Destroying the Competition: Sometimes a lawsuit has benefits beyond the immediate money your client can win. For example, a competitor might make an insignificant advertising mistake that allows a company to file a lawsuit and drive the competitor out of business.

The defendant in that case might not understand why the plaintiff is spending so much money when the potential monetary award will be small or the defendant is judgment proof. But for the plaintiff, closing down the competition could be invaluable.

Client mis-prediction: Clients make predictions, and their predictions can be wrong. When your client seems to be making decisions that are not justified by the math, explore his expectations to find the underlying assumptions. You might find a good reason for their approach, but you might find that your client has some funny ideas about how the judicial system works or how their opponent is likely to react to the case.

As tempting as it might be to let your client pursue an aggressive approach and fill your bank account, your job is to be a trusted advisor. Offer a reality check when it is needed, and follow it up in writing if your client resists your good advice.

•

MONEY VALUE

•

Early on, you must fully analyze the merits of the case, because this is the lens through which all decisions are rationalized. Too many clients and their lawyers throw random numbers around and then try to justify the numbers. They start with the number they want, and no matter what happens in the litigation, they stick with that number. Often a client or lawyer who is making this error will justify it by saying "a jury will go my way" or "we don't know how a jury will go, we're just as likely to win as the other side."

This is a huge error rooted in the Random Outcome Myth.

It is important to understand, and crucial that you explain to your clients, that damages must be justified to the fact finder. Generally, damages should reasonably compensate your client for his or her losses, making your client whole; not making your client better off than they were before they were wronged. Unfortunately, "being made whole" does not usually include the fees and costs of the litigation. In other words, for most clients it is impossible "to be made whole" because even if they get all of their damages, they still have to pay the expenses of the litigation.

As a rule of thumb, calculate the "Money Value" by taking the most likely award at trial and multiply it by a percentage between 20%-80%. If the plaintiff has a horrible case, use 20%; if they have nearly a sure-win, use 80%. You can assign any percentage in between and update as you go.

Of course, you can inflate the potential Money Value to huge proportions by adding punitive damages, pain and suffering, etc., and your client has probably read about a few big verdicts online before walking into your office.

But juries are made up of people, and although most clients think they are entitled to a lottery win, most people don't want to make other people rich just for the heck of it.

If you want more than you can credibly justify, your best bet is to have a very sympathetic client whose loss can be characterized as beyond money – they can't be made whole because of special circumstances, so no amount would truly be a windfall – or a defendant so horrible that the jury can be convinced that it is doing good work by taking money away from him.

Just showing that the defendant has a lot of money isn't going to move your jury unless you also have that sympathetic client, loss beyond money, and/or horrible defendant.

But most clients who believe they have a ten-million-dollar case simply don't fit into any special circumstances, and getting that client into a realistic damages range is crucial to negotiating a settlement and having a good outcome.

Don't be the lawyer who walks into mediation with a client who believes he has a 99% chance of winning three-million-dollars on an iffy $100,000 case.

•
Emotional Value
•

It has been said that there are six needs of victims. Whether you represent the plaintiff or the defendant, consider whether your client or the opposing party are actually seeking one or more of the following emotional results:

- Vengeance.

- Vindication (need to be right).

- Validation (need for respect and fairness).

- Need to create meaning.

- Need to be heard.

- Need for safety.

Addressing a combination of these emotional pillars creates "Emotional Value."

But Emotional Value is hard to calculate, and it must take into account the element of time. Is a $50,000 settlement now worth more to your client emotionally or is $60,000 better in three years?

This is not about a present-value calculation. This is about the stress of the next three years and the emotional satisfaction or lack thereof of the settlement now versus one three years from now.

CALCULATING A WIN

Once you separate – conceptually – the Goal Value, Money Value, and Emotional Value, you can work towards determining a "win."

It is important to determine what a "win" looks like: attorney's fees and costs frequently outsize the Money Value quickly.

If a case only has a potential maximum upside award of $50,000, it is nearly impossible to litigate on an hourly basis and make the math work. It could easily cost a client $20,000 before too long, which means that the client only has a potential "net" of $30,000 in the best-case scenario.

SKIPPING THE LEARNING CURVE

This sort of situation quickly leads to a "math trap" where the other side won't pay $50,000, because that is their worst-case scenario, but your client refuses to accept a $20,000 or even a $30,000 nuisance payment because it barely recoups his litigation expenses (or results in a loss on the endeavor). So, settlement is nearly impossible based solely on the math.

The math is always there and always a consideration. But a client will rationalize the math and the outcome if his goals and emotions are otherwise satisfied.

Of the three "value" variables, the hardest to quantify is Emotional Value. Is there ever enough money to compensate for the loss of a loved one or a limb?

Sometimes a plaintiff cannot "win" based on only Monetary Value, and all you can do is help your client to the best of your abilities.

Representing a defendant has a slightly different consideration than a plaintiff because a defendant can "win" by paying a lower amount than the full risk (which many defendants would not consider a win) or by having a high enough Emotional Value and/or Goal Value from the settlement or verdict.

Likewise, some defense cases you cannot win at all due to the nature of the claim. Cases involving practice areas such as employment, the ADA, the Clean Water Act, Class Actions, and others where the law has created outsized benefits to plaintiffs all create problems for defendants.

These are cases where it often costs more to fight the defense than to pay an early settlement.

Ironically, there can often (not always) be more pressure to settle these cases early if your defense is strong because fighting it increases expenses, a plaintiff's demand, and the risk of attorney's fees that your client may have to pay the other side in the case of a loss. Your client usually cannot get their own attorney's fees even if they win. This is because these cases are based in policy considerations, but are easy to abuse.

Even in these situations though, your client might consider the outcome a "win" if there is a high amount of Emotional Value or Goal Value.

Additionally, there can be a "win" by having a "smaller loss." For instance, if a defendant pays $70,000 in cumulate settlement and litigation expenses, but might have lost $300,000 at trial, then that is possibly a "win."

To win your cases, you should attempt to target these Values separately in order to increase or decrease them as appropriate. But always remember to frame any conversation in terms of money since that is the language of litigation.

•

THE PERSONALITIES AND MOTIVATIONS OF OPPOSING COUNSEL
•

Different lawyers have different business models and personalities. Understanding how the models interact with the personalities, and adjusting your approach accordingly, is a crucial skill. Let's start with the two basic business models, and the strengths and weaknesses of both.

BUSINESS MODELS

The legal industry has two basic business models. You might immediately think that these are "contingency fee" and "hourly," but that is not correct. Those are fee arrangements. The two models are the "delegation" model or the "DIY" model. Obviously, any individual law practice can be on a sliding scale between these, but generally law practices, regardless of size, tend to fall into these two models.

The Delegation Model

Description: In the delegation model, one lawyer, often (but not always) given the title "Partner," brings in the work, manages the clients, and tells other lawyers (or paralegals) what to do. These other lawyers might also have the title "Partner" or they might be called "Associates." Either way, the "delegation" style of practice is to separate the functions into marketers and workers.

A marketer's principal job function is to create work. In this style of practice, the marketers usually evaluate a case in the beginning and come up with their theory early on, but then they don't have time to re-evaluate or change the strategy and theory often. They also don't have time to review the actual evidence. Instead, they rely on summaries from the workers. The marketers have the ability to do very good work, but they don't have time.

Settlement Leverage Points and the Keystone of the Case

As mentioned above, this model can be found in all practice areas, in all size firms, and under any fee arrangement. For instance, a personal injury law firm can have a single lawyer and a team of paralegals. Or a larger firm can charge hourly and a Partner will have the Associates do most of the work. The primary characteristic to understand is the separation of key responsibilities into the marketers and the workers; those that bring in the work, and those that are assigned the bulk of the tasks.

Strengths: Practices operating under the delegation model usually have more resources available to spend on a case since some members of the practice are dedicated to doing the work. This is in contrast to a DIY model, where a lawyer has to spend time doing the work and everything else. A delegation model is easier to scale than a DIY model, especially in practice areas that have similar workflows and issues from one case to the next, such as personal injury.

Weaknesses: A delegation model can run into problems when the workers or resources of the firm get overwhelmed. More fundamentally, a delegation model often lacks focus, flexibility, and strategy in any specific lawsuit. Instead, it relies on forms and a cookie cutter approach in order to service a large number of cases. Frequently, a delegation model lacks transparency to the client: the pitch is that the marketer is a brilliant lawyer and is doing the work with support from the workers. But later, the client wonders why the workers are doing all the work, why the marketer is not available for communications, and why the workers are showing up at the hearings and not the marketer.

Motivations: Marketers must bring in work and make it profitable. They do not want to take risky strategies. Instead, they rely on approaches that they have used previously. As a result, they usually will conduct a large amount of discovery and bring motions to compel frequently. They don't want to be accused of having left a stone unturned.

The workers are either overworked, or else they are stressed out about not making their required billable hours. They tend to rely on the marketer's judgment about the merits of the case, in large part because marketers keep the workers in the dark as a deliberate strategy. The workers are the points of contact with opposing counsel, and the less a worker actually knows, the less information can leak to opposing counsel. Workers tend to develop a "team spirit" attitude, believing on faith that what the marketer tells them is correct.

DIY

Description: In the DIY model, the lawyer performs more of the work themselves. They often also maintain their own websites, arranges their own Powerpoint presentations, and does their trial preparation themselves. Often, they have good vendors that they can call on and delegate to when necessary. They may also have associates or other staff to help, but the amount of delegation is far less than in a delegation model.

While this is more common in smaller firms, there are a lot of large law firms whose individual partners practice this way. These, especially, can be very dangerous opponents because they have the resources usually unavailable to a DIY practice, but the strategic flexibility of a DIY practice.

Strengths: A lawyer operating under a DIY model will be more familiar with the details of the case. Because they are more involved in reviewing the evidence while also developing the theory and strategy, they are able to identify relevant details that would be frequently missed in a delegation model. A DIY model is also more flexible, resulting in more efficient use of the litigation budget. Sometimes a case will not need discovery in order to prove the case at trial, and a lawyer can show up for trial ready and willing to start voir dire. A lawyer under a delegation model would never dream of this. On the other hand, a DIY lawyer, having a full understanding of the case, would be more comfortable with this unorthodox approach.

Weaknesses: Lawyers operating under a DIY model may suffer in the quality of their work. Their papers are more prone to having typos or grammar mistakes if they don't have someone who can proofread and edit. Worse, they may be overwhelmed with office management issues and networking, and may rely on forms, templates, and habit in the same way that a delegation model does, thereby losing their strategic advantage.

Motivations: A DIY lawyer is motivated by saving money, both for themselves and their clients. They often have a higher volume of smaller cases, rather than fewer high-stakes cases. It can be harder to go to trial since there is less in-house support. The combination of time pressure and need to save money can lead to an urgency to settle cases.

PERSONALITIES

Like everyone else, different lawyers have different personalities. It can be helpful to try to classify your opponent in order to make generalizations and implement the best strategy.

There are three classifications that apply to the vast majority of lawyers you will encounter. Obviously, since these are generalizations, it is rare for a lawyer to fully encompass one of the classifications, and there are subtleties to a person's nature that this approach misses. But it is a helpful tool to use, especially at the start of the case when you have incomplete information about your opponent. All of these personality types can be found at any size or model firm.

The Firebreathing Pitbull

Description: This is the aggressive lawyer, often trying to "act like a lawyer." They usually don't fully analyze the merits of the case and just want to argue. They will waste their litigation budget on endless emails and phone calls that don't accomplish anything. They believe that "aggressive" advocacy means adopting an "aggressive" or hostile persona.

Do not ignore the Firebreathing Pitbull, but don't engage in their point-by-point letter writing campaigns or verbal battles. Focus on what you need for your case and preserve the record in case they later "exaggerate" the substance of your conversations to the judge. No matter how much they try to bait you, remain professional. Be especially mindful of your tone in written communications. In the heat of the moment, it is easy to shoot off a sarcastic email that will make you say "haha, take that!" But such victories are pyrrhic. The Firebreathing Pitbull won't ever feel like they lost, and a judge will look at you on the same level as your opponent. It is far better for a judge to view you as the mature and professional person you are.

At the same time, do not become a pushover by trying to avoid being (or aggravating) a Firebreathing Pitbull. There is a difference between an aggressive personality and aggressive litigation tactics. If you find yourself imitating the stereotypical television lawyer, then you are heading down the wrong path. But using aggressive *tactics*, especially when you do so without resorting to Firebreathing Pitbull style threats and grandstanding, is very effective.

Strengths: A Firebreathing Pitbull often can bully their way into favorable results, as long as those results are not given by a judge or jury. They rely on their opponent being intimidated or having less stamina for confrontation. Often this can provide an advantage in the beginning and middle stages of a lawsuit.

Weaknesses: The Firebreathing Pitbull is overwhelmed by their own ego. They are under the assumption that because they have more years of practice, or a large dollar value of settlements, or the characteristics of any other myth (see Common and Persistent Myths in Part II) that they will win. And so, they miscalculate the merits of the case. They have a tendency to see only their side, and no counterargument. Because they never compromise, they create hostility with their counterparts, and end up causing needless expense on both sides.

Motivations: Fueled by ego, the Firebreathing Pitbull needs to "feel" like they win every email exchange or conversation. If they lose a motion or a trial, they will blame the judge or the jury. They will engage in endless and pointless fights in order to get the last word or prove that they won't back down. They will object at depositions just to make the process more difficult. The Firebreathing Pitbull is happier losing a motion to compel and paying sanctions than cooperating.

SKIPPING THE LEARNING CURVE

The Incompetent

Description: Unfortunately, you will sometimes run into an opposing counsel that simply doesn't know the facts of their case or can't properly analyze the law. They don't know what they're doing and often compensate by adopting a non-cooperative attitude. Certainly, Firebreathing Pitbulls may also be Incompetents, but the true Incompetent does not have the time or ability to do a good job; a Firebreathing Pitbull can analyze and argue well, but mistakenly thinks doing a good job means being hostile.

An Incompetent may not be "incompetent" to the point that would merit disbarment, but it can be difficult to have productive discussions with someone that will not – or cannot – look at evidence or properly apply it to the law. Your best approach against an Incompetent is to prepare for summary judgment or trial. You should understand from the start that settlement will be difficult, or not the best available outcome.

Two notes of caution: First, a true Incompetent will often act hostile out of a lack of confidence. Thus, you may mischaracterize an Incompetent as a Firebreathing Pitbull. But an Incompetent and a Firebreathing Pitbull are different. Their strengths, weaknesses, and motivations are different. And so your approach to each must be different.

Second, don't assume that every lawyer that disagrees with you or refuses to concede a point is an Incompetent. Reasonable minds can disagree. Other times, they have to placate their client and are just doing their job. Don't forget that a lawyer's interaction with their client affects their interaction with you!

And, on occasion, opposing counsel will disagree with you because they're correct and you're wrong (much less likely if you follow the advice in this book).

Strengths: An Incompetent will often have a scattershot approach to litigation, thereby making it expensive for both sides. Since they are not properly reasoning through the case, settlement can be difficult. More often than not, if one side is unreasonable and the other side is reasonable, then the unreasonable party gets a better deal.

Weaknesses: An Incompetent drives up their own expenses as well as those of the opposing party. Their writing and arguments are lackluster. Although their cases often involve a large amount of law and motion, they frequently lose. Their written arguments tend to rely heavily on pasted verbiage from practice guides and overemphasize the law, while neglecting to thoroughly apply the facts. They also ignore practical and policy concerns.

Motivations: Incompetents like to stay in their comfort zones. They want to use arguments and strategies that they have seen before. Incompetents are likely to do things "because that's how they have always been done."

The Strategist

Description: This is the kind of lawyer you want to be. The Strategist might pretend to be a Firebreathing Pitbull or an Incompetent when it's convenient, or they might be reasonable and cooperative. Strategists have a strong ability to analyze and argue the law, but they are not infallible. However, unlike Firebreathing Pitbulls or Incompetents, Strategists can see the other side's arguments, thereby often feeling insecure in their position.

Strengths: Strategists have a more objective view of their cases, thereby being able to craft more convincing arguments and more effective approaches. Strategists view a "win" more broadly, and so they are more conscientious of the litigation budget. While often still having an ego, Strategists acknowledge that a good outcome is not guaranteed.

Weaknesses: Strategists can be insecure due to their ability to see weaknesses in their case. Sometimes this can lead them to temper their strong arguments more than necessary or be unduly passive, especially when dealing with a Firebreathing Pitbull.

Motivations: Strategists want the best outcome for their client, which does not necessarily mean "winning" at trial. Sometimes this can lead to early friction between a Strategist and their client since the Strategist will explain the weaknesses, but the client will mistake that for a lack of confidence in the case.

IN SUMMARY

By classifying your opponent's business model and personality, you can adapt your communications and strategy to exploit their weaknesses.

You also need to have enough self-awareness to understand your own business model and personality so that your opponent does not have an unseen advantage over you.

KEYSTONE/LEVERAGE POINTS

Once you identify your opponent's practice and personality type, you then need to determine the "Keystone" of the case. The Keystone is something (sometimes multiple things) that, once discovered, can quickly resolve a case without regard to the legal merits. It is surprising how many cases actually have Keystones and how large the leverage can be once you discover one. But it is not enough to just discover the Keystone. You also have to know how to use it.

Here are some of the most common Keystones that arise frequently:

The Deep Dark Secret

One side or the other often has a Deep Dark Secret. It may be that they did not tell their spouse that they are involved in a lawsuit. Or it might be that they don't actually have the budget for litigation and were hoping to settle quickly. Maybe an ongoing lawsuit could blow up a potential business deal, damage a relationship or reputation, or cause health-threatening stress levels.

You must try to figure out your client's Deep Dark Secret before it comes out on its own. That way, it is not a surprise and you can have time to figure out how to deal with it. A Deep Dark Secret always gets revealed even if it's not directly relevant to the case.

SKIPPING THE LEARNING CURVE

If you can figure out the other party's Deep Dark Secret, you can take advantage of it and this will often cause a case to settle. For instance, if you realize that the other party did not tell their spouse that they are involved in a lawsuit, then threatening to depose the spouse (if allowed) will apply a large amount of pressure. If you discover that the other party has a low tolerance for stress, or doesn't have time to deal with the lawsuit, scheduling their deposition and sending discovery that their lawyers will need their input on will apply pressure.

OPPOSING COUNSEL'S MALPRACTICE

Sometimes the opposing counsel will make a critical error. They might have named the wrong plaintiff (an individual and not the entity, or vice versa), or they might have missed a deadline. Instead of hammering them with the fact and causing them to be defensive, reveal this in subtle ways where they think you might not know. They won't want their client to know, so they will encourage settlement on terms favorable to your side in order to cover up their mistake. And, if you don't tell them outright, then it will become too late for them to fix the problem and you can use it in Summary Judgment.

OPPOSING PARTY'S OR COUNSEL'S FEAR OF TRIAL

Often a party will be scared to go to trial. Likewise, many lawyers are scared as well. In the case of a lawyer, this fear is not always consistent with their level of experience.

Settlement Leverage Points and the Keystone of the Case

It is not uncommon to find a less experienced attorney with no fear of trial, or a seasoned litigator with a crippling fear of putting a case to a jury. Regardless of the reason for the fear, if it exists in your opponent or the other party, you will gain significant leverage as you approach trial. Often, it can be the impending trial date that triggers settlement.

OPPOSING PARTY'S OR COUNSEL'S FINANCES

A party that cannot afford the litigation obviously is more inclined to settle. But sometimes, such as in contingency cases, it is not the party's expenses that gives you leverage (since in contingency cases the party typically does not pay costs up front), but rather their need for money *now*.

Likewise, opposing counsel might be more inclined to talk their client into settling early, for less value, if their client has run out of money to pay them or if they themselves otherwise need a quick contingency payoff.

POTENTIAL FALLOUT

Sometimes there could be a finding in your matter that causes one side problems going forward. For instance, if you represent a client who was treated as an independent contractor, and your lawsuit alleges that she was misclassified and should have been an employee, then a finding of misclassification can cause other, similar contractors to be reclassified. The defendant in such a case would not want that finding and would be encouraged to settle early.

There are many other issues that you may be able to discover. Never forget that it is unethical and often illegal to expressly demand a settlement in exchange for not revealing them. But that doesn't mean the issues don't exist, and it doesn't mean that the other side is not already thinking about them.

TRUE STORY

We represented a client in an arbitration involving a very small contract dispute. Early on we realized that the defendant's business model was possibly illegal. Because there was so little in dispute, if the other side fought at all, then it would not have been worth pursuing.

Instead, we convinced the other side that we don't need discovery and we should have the arbitration on the briefs only. We pitched it as an approach that made sense for both sides since it was a silly little dispute and the defendant was represented by a big firm, so they might as well save money too.

They were happy to agree.

We won the arbitration in an Interim Award, and explained that we were going to move to confirm the Award as soon as it was finalized.

This resulted in a four-figure case turning into a six-figure settlement.

Throwing a Monkey Wrench

Often, the process of a lawsuit is relatively predictable. But sometimes derailing the other side's expectations can upset the balance so much that it creates a lot of settlement pressure. One easy example is by creating a more complex lawsuit out of a simple one.

Most plaintiffs go into a lawsuit with an idea in their heads about how it will go (e.g., "once they see the lawsuit they will pay up instead of paying a lawyer.") Surprising them with a cross-complaint, or otherwise creating uncertainty in the facts will often provide a lot of leverage.

There are often facts and arguments that you can use to create uncertainty even though they aren't the strongest points you have. This might provide the basis for a cross-complaint that you can use for leverage or to conduct discovery that you otherwise wouldn't be able to.

Filing a cross-complaint also locks the plaintiff into litigating a case that they may otherwise have thought they could abandon at any time.

Your goal is not to prove that your interpretation or theory here is correct or to try to use weak allegations to negotiate a better settlement. Your goal is to create leverage by opening up procedural tools that would not otherwise have been available.

Obviously, this discovery can also help prove your case, which is why it is permissible. And you should not discount the evidentiary value that can be gained.

Don't be confused into thinking the purpose is to engage in abusive litigation tactics or frivolous cross-complaints. The point is that these areas of exploration often provide a lot of leverage because opposing counsel, and their client, did not expect it.

This can be especially effective against a delegation model practice where the attorneys expect and rely on lawsuits following familiar and predictable routines.

Here are a couple common avenues of attack to Throw a Monkey Wrench:

- **Important terms in a contract:** A creative attorney can explain why either party would be in breach in nearly any dispute involving a written agreement (even more so an oral agreement). What does "X" really mean anyway?

- **Intent:** in any dispute, intent often comes up. The intent of the parties or witnesses is often a fact that can be disputed and create uncertainty that can be leveraged.

EXERCISE

Try this exercise to help recognize the Keystone concept in practice:

- Identify a past case that you settled that ended far better or far worse than expected.

- Can you identify a Keystone that affected the settlement that you only discovered towards the end or after the case?

- In thinking back on the case, can you now identify any hints about the existence of the Keystone?

- Can you now identify any other Keystones that you could have identified while litigating the case?

- If you knew about the Keystones at the beginning of the case, how would you have done things differently?

PART IV

STRATEGIES AND COUNTERSTRATEGIES

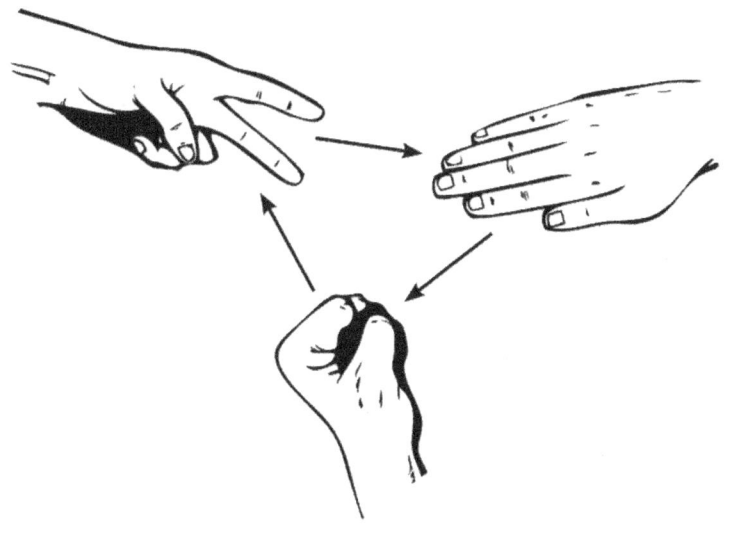

Strategies and Counterstrategies

The Tale of the Wise Old Partner

"The legal team was distraught.

They were about to start trial in a case that had been litigated for over three years, and they felt they had no chance since they were up against a much larger firm with more resources. The lead partner could tell that if his team approached trial so depressed and dour, it would not play well to the jury. If they were enthusiastic and optimistic, they would have a shot since the law and facts were on their side.

Before the first day of trial, he gathered his team in a conference room. With all eyes on him, he said 'I have this coin that was passed down through my family for generations and has always accurately predicted how my trials would go. I know most of you are not superstitious, and I don't know why it works, but it has never failed. When I flip it, if it's heads, it means we will definitely win, if it's tails, we will definitely lose.' With that, he tossed the coin in the air. All of the lawyers watched intently as it bounced and rattled on the conference room table, and eventually came to rest heads up.

The room erupted in a cheer. Energized, the team went on to win their trial.

On the way out of the courthouse, an associate turned to the partner and said 'I wish I had a magic coin like that.' The partner said 'here, take mine, I have a drawer full.'

The associate looked at the coin, and, speechless, realized it was a novelty two-headed quarter."

> *"Engage people with what they expect; it is what they are able to discern and confirms their projections. It settles them into predictable patterns of response, occupying their minds while you wait for the extraordinary moment — that which they cannot anticipate."*
>
> *– Sun Tzu*

You will hear the buzz-phrase "litigation strategy" come up frequently. But it is difficult to find information about what that means. A lot of lawyers will define their strategy as "preparing for trial from day one" or "taking depositions before sending written discovery" or "always filing a demurrer." These might be aspects of a broader strategy, but they do not define an actual strategy.

In this section, I describe multiple strategies that you can apply and information on how to counter them. You should not latch on to one or two. Rather, by using the tools and techniques from earlier, you will be able to implement the strategy that best applies in any given situation. And you should be flexible so that you can shift from one strategy to another as the case evolves.

This is not an exhaustive list of all strategies. But these strategies – organized into "communication" strategies and "case" strategies – will get you thinking strategically, so that you can formulate and recognize strategies in your own practice.

Communication strategies are those that relay a message to the other side.

Case strategies are those that deal with actions that relate to the case.

These two broad categories – communication and case strategies – are two distinct aspects to any given litigation, and each must be understood as separate and also affecting the other.

Each list is further broken down into "common" and "uncommon" strategies. I don't have statistics to back these claims up – this is anecdotal, based on what I have experienced in my practice – but it is no coincidence that the common strategies are easier to implement. Whether these are called "common/uncommon," "beginner/advanced," or "easy/hard," is not important. The point is that you should know that you will more often have opposing counsel utilize the "common" ones, and by virtue of being more common, they are easier to counter. That's not to say they are "worse" or that you should never use them. To the contrary: if you use a strategy that your opponent is familiar with, they will instinctively classify you in their mind as "that kind of lawyer," which creates opportunities for you to gain an advantage.

Think of these strategies as tools in your toolbox. You want to use the right one for the right situation: effective litigation strategy means implementing the strategy deliberately. It also means using it consistently in order to communicate to your opponent (or through your opponent to their client) the proper message – whatever message you have chosen to communicate. But don't be afraid to suddenly switch strategies if one is not working or, tactically, to shake things up once your opponent believes you have become predictable.

For instance, you can surprise your opponent by using settlement discussions as a Decoy, so that neither side propounds discovery, while actually Plowing Ahead and preparing for trial. If settlement discussions "fail" when it is too late to do discovery, you will be prepared for trial and your opponent will not be. But be cognizant of the fallout in such a strategy: you will also not have propounded discovery, you will increase hostilities, and your opponent will run into court to try to get a trial extension (a lot of judges will not be sympathetic to your opponent in such circumstances, but some may be). That is just one example.

In using these strategies, your goal should never be to "convince" the other side that they will lose. Even if they have doubts about their case, no one will ever admit it, and far too many lawyers are immune to doubt. Instead, you have three simpler goals: (1) gather as much information as possible, (2) raise doubts in your opponent's mind (without care for whether they confess those doubts to you or not), and (3) change the math.

COMMON COMMUNICATION STRATEGIES

Plenty of books, blog posts, and articles explain the technical aspects of being a lawyer that I touched upon previously. But at the heart of these technical skills are communication strategies.

Strategies and Counterstrategies

You will communicate with your client, with the judge, with the jury, and with your opposing counsel. And that last category of communication – with your opposing counsel – has the potential to make or break your case. The way you behave in those interactions can determine how much information you get, how much time and money you spend to get it, whether your case settles and for how much, and what kind of reputation you carry into your next case and the ones after that.

It is easy to fall into certain communication traps as a lawyer. Everyone does it at some point, either because we have a belief about how lawyers are "supposed to act," or because we work in a profession that constantly throws new and difficult situations at us.

These first communication strategies are those that are common. No matter which communication strategy you employ, remember that communication strategies are most effective if used consistently, so that your opponent believes you are predictable. But then you can make strategic changes at the right time to gain an advantage.

Just Say No

Description: "Just Say No" may be the most common communication strategy implemented by lawyers.

It can be tempting, as an advocate working one side of a dispute, to reject everything your counterpart suggests. The Just Say No strategy can be very effective… if your goal is to make the litigation time consuming, expensive, and frustrating for both sides.

As a Just Say No lawyer you will succeed at wasting your opponent's time and money, and you won't risk agreeing to a deal that benefits your adversary. But you will also increase animosity, making it more difficult to collaborate if collaboration becomes beneficial to your client later.

You also risk rejecting ideas that could be good for both sides, and you turn yourself into a very predictable opponent.

In fact, the predictability is probably the biggest pitfall to utilizing this strategy. I have lost count of the number of times I have offered opposing counsel compromises that would have benefited their case because I knew they would reject it out of hand.

This results in my opponent taking weak positions and creating a paper-trail that comes back to haunt them simply because they say "no" without thinking. If they had been strategic, they would have accepted some of these proposals. And then I would have fallen into their trap instead of the other way around.

Although it is easy and sometimes effective to be a Just Say No lawyer, it is rarely the most effective way to win your client's case.

Counter: What should you do if you are litigating against a Just Say No lawyer? Use the predictability against him as we did in the example below!

Pros:
- Easy to implement.

- Does not require research or knowledge of the case.

Strategies and Counterstrategies

- Avoids making concessions that could later turn out to have been wrong choices.

- Shifts decision-making to the judge and provides a strong defense against a later malpractice case brought against you.

- Often frustrating, time consuming, and expensive to Counter.

- Gives the false (but comforting) impression to your clients and to yourself that you are an "aggressive" litigator.

- Increases litigation fees and costs for both parties.

Cons:
- Predictable.

- Common.

- Easy to Counter even though it is often frustrating, time consuming, and expensive to do so.

- Lack of a broader goal.

- Lack of effectiveness at helping to win your case on the merits.

- Increases animosity.

- High risk of losing out on favorable compromises.

- Weakens overall case position more often than strengthening it due to wasted expenses on non-beneficial work, leaving a lower budget for higher-return efforts.

- More likely to lead to a fee-dispute with your client.

- Increases litigation fees and costs for both parties.

TRUE STORY

We represented the Plaintiff in a case alleging multiple causes of action, including Breach of Fiduciary Duty. The Defendants threatened to demur to the complaint. The Breach of Fiduciary Duty was a weak theory, much weaker than our Breach of Contract or other causes of action. I offered to dismiss the one cause of action, without prejudice, in exchange for them not bringing a demurrer. I acknowledged that it was a weak, although viable, theory.

I even explained that if they file a demurrer, we will oppose, and I thought we would win. So they might as well save everyone's time and money and accept our proposal, since they were highly unlikely to win their demurrer on any cause of action.

Opposing counsel in this case had already demonstrated that they use a "Just Say No" strategy, so we didn't think they would accept our offer. And if they did, we would not have lost anything because the case would still go forward.

Predictably, they said "No" and demanded that we dismiss the entire complaint. In the end, they brought a demurrer to the entire complaint and we opposed. The judge went our way and we got to keep Breach of Fiduciary Duty. And because the judge's tentative acknowledged that the claims could support a Fiduciary relationship – which was questionable – we were able to point to that for the rest of the case.

Their stubborn and predictable strategy made the weakest part of our case stronger, and the already strong aspects even stronger still!

Confrontation

Description: Closely related to the "Just Say No" strategy, it can be tempting to take a Confrontational approach. After all, litigation is a contest and you're in it to win!

In a Confrontational communication strategy, you don't wait for your opponent to request a concession. Instead, you actively threaten increased battles – whether or not you intend to follow through. For instance, upon receiving discovery responses, you might send a letter saying that the responses are wholly inadequate before even flipping through them.

But a Confrontational strategy, like any one-dimensional approach to communication, can do more harm than good. As a Confrontational lawyer, you will turn everything into an argument. Sometimes, that will be beneficial to your client. And it will certainly make the case more difficult for your opponent. But, like the Just Say No strategy, you will leave good deals on the table by resisting every effort at cooperation. And a Confrontational approach will either exhaust you or become your personality, neither one of which is a good outcome for you!

If you have a Confrontational attitude, be aware of your natural tendencies. Then, instead of allowing that Confrontational energy to control your approach, try to direct it to the places where it will have the most impact. Spend time to decide where you can't give an inch and where you have room to move, not just in settlement discussions but in discovery and motions. And know when to cooperate.

Strategies and Counterstrategies

But Confrontation can also be necessary in order to avoid being run over by a hostile opponent. You need to know when to utilize it and when not to.

Easier said than done, right? A good rule of thumb is to always start your relationship with your opponent with as much courtesy and cooperation as you can. Grant any reasonable requests that will not do real damage to your client... but the minute your opponent fails to respond with the same courtesy, stop giving until courtesy is restored.

Keep a separate document of "requests," and "agreements." If you make a request for an extension or some other professional courtesy, you should write it in the table and keep track of whether or not it was granted. Make sure you keep the scores roughly even and let the other side know if they are being one sided. There are plenty of lawyers who believe they should "always take, never give." Amazingly, they even get offended when you don't give courtesies in response.

But mind the difference between being cooperative and being milquetoast.

Counter: Like the Just Say No strategy, the Confrontation strategy is easy to implement and easy to counter. The counter is the same as countering the Just Say No strategy, but requires a little more planning. The counter to this is to ask for a reasonable trade, where what you are offering would benefit the opposing side but what you are requesting is actually relatively unimportant to you.

If you are up against a lawyer implementing this strategy, then you are likely to need to go to court on motions to compel, or defending against them. Creating a record demonstrating that you are reasonable also means that you are far more likely to win your motions, and even get an uncourteous opposing counsel sanctioned.

A word of caution: a lot of lawyers believe that the counter to this strategy is to implement it themselves, and to be even more Confrontational. This does not work. It leads to a very large waste of time and money on needless bickering and causes you to lose track of the bigger picture.

Another great counter is to focus some discovery requests on documents and information that benefits the other side. They won't turn it over and will say "go ahead and compel." These documents and information can later become the subject of a motion in-limine. A lot of judges won't let a party bring in evidence at trial if they refused to turn it over, whether or not you have compelled (but be careful assuming this, because other judges will not exclude evidence if you have not tried to compel production first).

Pros:
- Easy to implement.

- Does not require research or knowledge of the case.

- Avoids making concessions that could later turn out to have been wrong.

- Shifts decision-making to the judge and provides a strong defense against a later malpractice case brought against you.

- Often frustrating, time consuming, and expensive to counter.

- Gives the false, but comforting, impression both to clients and yourself that you are an "aggressive" litigator.

- Increases litigation fees and costs for both parties.

Cons:

- Predictable; common.

- Easy to counter even though it is often frustrating, time consuming, and expensive to do so.

- Lack of broader goal.

- Lack of effectiveness at helping to win your case on the merits.

- Increases animosity.

- High risk of losing out on favorable compromises.

- Weakens overall case position more often than strengthening it due to wasted expenses on non-beneficial work, leaving a lower budget for higher-return efforts.

- More likely to lead to a fee-dispute with your client.

- Increases litigation fees and costs for both parties.

SKIPPING THE LEARNING CURVE

TRUE STORY

In a case where the "value" of products was a central issue, we propounded discovery responses seeking invoices related to comparable products sold by the same company.

We knew opposing counsel would threaten to seek a protective order or force us to compel. But, we also knew that those invoices would be beneficial to the other party's case, and we had alternatives if we did not get the information. We created a paper-trail explaining why we wanted the information, and they created a paper-trail explaining why it was completely irrelevant. We did not compel.

At mediation they argued that the invoices – that they refused to turn over – would be very beneficial to them at trial. In a joint session with the mediator and opposing counsel, but not the clients, I pointed out that they had created a paper-trail that would allow us to keep the invoices out of trial with a motion in-limine. Opposing counsel's eyes told the whole story. Less than two hours later the case settled on terms very favorable to our client.

I have no idea if the judge would have granted the motion in-limine.

KNOW IT ALL

Description: Another tempting behavioral trap that many of us fall into, especially when dealing with an opponent, is to answer everything with assertive confidence whether or not we actually know the answer.

Strategies and Counterstrategies

As a Know It All lawyer, you may be persuasive and intimidating, but you are also taking a risk. The Know It All lawyer always has the answer... but it isn't necessarily the right answer or the best answer, and, by speaking before you think, you might give away more information than you should.

The fear shared by many lawyers is that if you don't quickly and immediately answer, then you appear as if you don't know what you're doing or as if you don't believe in your case, and "something bad" will happen.

But if you don't know the answer to something when you're talking to opposing counsel, that usually doesn't matter. If you find yourself falling into this habit, take a deep breath and relax. You don't always have to be the first one to speak. In fact, you don't always have to speak at all.

Make a point of saying "I'll look into it and get back to you" when you haven't had a chance to do your research, review the relevant documents, talk to your client, or think about your strategy. Then do your homework and return with the best answer, instead of the fastest or loudest one. You'll find that your actual confidence goes up, your stress levels go down, and people start to trust and value your input more. And, once you are free from the trap of believing you have to know everything all the time, you can deploy the persuasion and intimidation aspects of the Know It All lawyer when it is the best approach, and not because it is your default approach.

Counter: If you are dealing with a Know It All Lawyer, don't be intimidated, you're probably just as smart and prepared as the Know It All. Don't let him pressure you – feel free to take your time, do your research, and think about what you want to say, even if your opponent doesn't want you to. Verify everything the Know It All Lawyer tells you, no matter how convincing it sounded in the moment.

And remember their weakness: often, a Know It All is compensating for a lack of confidence, knowledge, or ability. So give this opponent an opportunity to talk. People who are insecure want to talk to prove that they know what they're doing. Other times, the Know It All is overconfident and sees you as no threat. Consequently, they patronize and want to intimidate.

Whatever the cause, a Know It All is likely to speak without thinking, and will often share information that they shouldn't!

Pros:
- Can sometimes cause your opponent not to independently research and analyze an issue.

- Can create doubt in your opponent.

- Easy to implement.

Cons:
- Lack of broader goal.

- Lack of preparation.

- Lack of effectiveness at helping to win your case on the merits.

TRUE STORY

In a case where opposing counsel was threatening to demur to a cause of action for Fraud, I asked whether the issue was one of specificity or whether they disagreed with the legal theory. They responded "both" and went on at length, and vehemently, about why it fails. It became clear that opposing counsel had a muddied understanding of the difference between a factual allegation and a legal theory.

Instead of debating the issues – which would be pointless against a Know It All because they will never concede a point – I simply said "I disagree, I think you should file your demurrer." Predictably, the demurrer was a mess and conflated allegations and legal theory. Result: we won, demurrer overruled.

Although the result of the demurrer was predictable, we used the knowledge of them being a Know It All to our advantage. Their demurrer, combined with the information they leaked in our phone calls, allowed us to thoroughly outline any possible legal theory they might be able to use at trial (and without even having to draw this out in discovery.)

This information was invaluable to shaping our case and they had no idea why things went downhill for them so fast for the rest of the case. The conversation quickly went from them saying that their client "will never settle" to them saying their client "will never get a fair hearing in front of this judge, so we have to settle." To which I said "I guess we're just lucky," even though I had been leading them down a specific path the whole time.

Hopefully, they don't read this book....

Uncommon Communication Strategies

These next communication strategies are "uncommon." You will come across these less often. As a consequence, your opponents will also be less familiar with them.

Play Dumb

Description: There is nothing more frustrating than dealing with an opposing counsel that simply does not "get it," such as when dealing with an Incompetent. But you don't need to be Incompetent to pretend to be.

As lawyers, we are used to asking tough questions. In general, you are more likely to get opposing counsel talking if you ask innocently. People want to be understood and will do the work to make you understand them. If you keep asking for explanations with a tone of genuine confusion or curiosity, you will often get answers!

And keeping quiet can have the same effect – never underestimate the human desire to fill empty space with words. So next time you're tempted to ask a confrontational question, consider whether you might do better with a curious one. And don't be quick to jump in to make your point or end a conversation – you might accomplish more with a few beats of silence.

Counter: If you think opposing counsel is Playing Dumb in order to get information from you, turn it around! Ask questions like "Why do you ask?" or "Is there a particular part of this issue that isn't clear?" or "Help me understand where the confusion is?"

This will force your "confused" counterpart to give you information, and will buy you a little time to think about how much information you actually want to share. Make a point of thinking before you speak. You don't have to ramble on in response to a confused opponent, and you definitely don't have to fill every silence with chatter. Resisting these impulses will serve you well in most interactions.

Pros:

- Can get a lot of information with little work.

- Can lead to your opponent underestimating you.

- Can create a genuinely cooperative atmosphere if the other attorney is friendly.

Cons:

- If you Play Dumb too well or often, your opponent could lose respect for you, causing you to lose leverage.

- Can cause you to be unprepared while thinking you are doing so "strategically."

> **TRUE STORY**
>
> A company was using our client's trademarks in their metatags. We sent a cease-and-desist letter to get them to stop. This initiated a series of discussions with their lawyer, who was claiming that it had nothing to do with our client. Even though I understood how search engines work, I kept Playing Dumb by saying things like "our client seems to think this is a big deal, but I don't get all this technical mumbo jumbo."
>
> The other attorney, frustrated by my lack of understanding, spent a long time on the phone with me going through how metatags help drive searches, not realizing that he was proving our point. This let me then follow up with a draft complaint sent to him using his own explanation against him (see Always Leave Room for Escalation).
>
> They took down the infringing metatags shortly after without us having to file a lawsuit.

Decoy

Description: There are a lot of ways to use small issues, weak points, and misdirection to your advantage. You may decide to save the best caselaw for court or mediation, instead of including them in an early letter to opposing counsel. Or you might lead your opponent to believe that a non-issue is very important to your client in order to set up a better settlement later.

Strategies and Counterstrategies

Likewise, you might allow your opponent to control early discussions in order to hold back your strongest points until a more strategic moment. Take advantage of the "Just Say No" lawyer with this strategy – he will easily fall into the trap of taking the opposite side of whatever issue you raise, whether not that is the issue you should really be dealing with.

For instance, if there's a question of whether a contract is binding and it would be in your best interests for the contract to be binding, make opposing counsel think that you want the contract *not* to be binding. That way they will argue that it actually is binding just because their strategy is to take the opposite position. You may wonder whether opposing counsel will really take a position that hurts their case simply because they think you don't want them to take that position. The short answer: yes, often they will.

This strategy is also highly effective to control a disorganized opponent.
If your opponent sends a request for production that is overly broad, make it clear that you are withholding irrelevant documents. Your opponent will fight tooth and nail for those documents, thinking that you are withholding crucial information. Fight just as hard to withhold the documents. Make them compel. Some common boilerplate that you should expect to see is language such as "if they have nothing to hide, they wouldn't be fighting so hard." Then, when you finally turn over the documents, expect a very angry phone call from your opponent accusing you (rightly) of wasting their time and their client's money fighting for something irrelevant. In the meantime, you have successfully caused them to ignore the useful evidence that you *actually* turned over.

Counter: It can be difficult to identify if your opponent is using a Decoy, particularly because it is so rarely employed even though it can be extremely effective. The best counter is to follow the techniques outlined in Part II of this book and prepare your case from the start.

If you are well organized, well prepared, and confident in your abilities, then your counterpart's Decoys will not affect you. Don't assume that the other side is taking the best approach or making the best argument for their case. If you make that assumption, you will focus too much on opposing their case instead of making yours.

While their arguments are important, you should arrive at your position independently and not merely for the sake of opposing theirs (unless you are doing that as a deliberate strategy).

Pros:
- Can lead your opponent to make the argument that you are most prepared to deal with.

- Retains flexibility for future choices.

- Extremely effective when used properly.

- Can lead to your opponent underestimating you.

Cons:
- Can be hard to execute well – you have to think carefully and think ahead in order to get the results you want.

- Can create unnecessary discussion and wasted time on irrelevant and unproductive issues.

Strategies and Counterstrategies

> **TRUE STORY**
>
> We had a case where the other side threatened to bring a demurrer. During the meet and confer process, it was clear that they were going to bring it no matter what. We wanted them to focus on a specific issue that we knew was stronger for us, so we took a quote from a Dissent in a case that supported our position. The same rule could have been taken from the main opinion of a different case, but we wanted them to focus on that issue since we knew it was strong for us.
>
> In my conversation with opposing counsel, she said "that is from a Dissent and is not binding." I said "we think it's persuasive even though it's from a Dissent." This successfully lured them into filing a Demurrer focusing on that issue (I assume they thought they were being clever and pre-empting our argument). In our Opposition, we did not rely on the Dissent. Instead, we used the binding opinion of a different case. Easy win.

ALWAYS LEAVE ROOM FOR ESCALATION

Description: This is one of the most powerful strategies, but one of the least used. Often, especially in settlement negotiations, an attorney will lay out their entire case to justify their first anchoring number. This is a devastating mistake because their subsequent negotiations rely on everything they have already said.

Instead, during negotiations, hold back evidence and arguments so that you can escalate while simultaneously making your case stronger.

This strategy is also extremely effective in other aspects of litigation. What you say, and the number of things you say at one time, does not have a strong impact. Instead, the number of times you are able to effectively respond with new information, especially if you can escalate with stronger positions, is what matters.

Counter: If someone is using escalation in a negotiation with you, try to figure out what they are withholding: is it facts, evidence, or legal theories? Consider the negotiation stage an information gathering mission. Avoid numbers as much as you can while asking for more information – they want to ration it out and may be persuaded to do so even if you aren't making many moves. If they are escalating their threats, consider calling their bluff. They probably don't want to go straight to their most aggressive option (that's why they are escalating), so forcing them into it early can put them off balance.

Pros:

- Avoids being backed into a corner in negotiations, because you will always be planning your path forward.

- Strengthens your negotiating position since you always have more "moves" available than your opponent.

Cons:

- Only works if your opponent is negotiating.

- Won't get you anywhere with a non-responsive opponent, because you won't have an opportunity to escalate.

Strategies and Counterstrategies

> **TRUE STORY**
>
> We frequently write demand letters that only briefly describe the facts and do not include a draft complaint. This often triggers a detailed and lengthy response from the other side. We then have more information and can "escalate" by providing some more facts and explanation, escalate again with evidence, and escalate yet again by providing a draft complaint.
>
> This leaves the other side little room to counter.
>
> But it's important to remember that demand letters should not be boilerplate, generalized, or vague. If they are not detailed enough or are clearly form letters then they have little value (unless you just need to satisfy a notice requirement and are not looking to negotiate a settlement).

•
COMMON CASE STRATEGIES
•

Like communication strategies, you have a number of options in how you approach ongoing litigation. Don't fall into the bad habit of doing things "because that's how they've always been done." You can – and should – litigate deliberately and strategically.

Attrition

Description: Attrition is often the reason a case settles. Usually, attorneys on both sides litigate without focus. As a result, the expenses on both sides get out of control, leading both sides to want to settle. But Attrition can be purposely used by turning everything into a battle. This is the most natural follow-through strategy to a Confrontation approach. But like that strategy, it should rarely be used because it is scattershot and does not focus on winning on the merits.

This strategy is most effective if one side has a much larger litigation budget than the other and a broader goal than just winning this particular case.

Counter: Attrition can be difficult to counter if it is being used correctly, and it can be devastating to a client without an adequate litigation budget. But it only works if the attorney using it has a big budget; if not, the attorney's choice to attempt to win through Attrition is a double-edged sword.

To counter Attrition, you should plan to make concessions, particularly in the "meet and confer" process. Focus on efficiency, and ignore opposing counsel's animosity and aggression. Bait them into wasting their time while you prepare for trial. Since they will try to turn everything into a motion, you have to take away their ability to do so. In most cases, Attrition is used poorly, resulting in the other side running through their litigation budget too early in a case.

Strategies and Counterstrategies

Pros:

- Difficult to counter. Also, it may be particularly difficult for opposing counsel to counter without behaving poorly.

- Often leads to a settlement that is a loss for both parties, with no clear winner.

- Easy to implement.

- Does not require research or knowledge of the case.

- Avoids making concessions that could later turn out to have been wrong.

- Shifts decision-making to the judge and provides a strong defense against a later malpractice case brought against you.

- Often frustrating, time consuming, and expensive to counter.

- Gives the false, but comforting, impression to clients and to yourself that you are an "aggressive" litigator.

- Increases litigation fees and costs for both parties.

Cons:

- Expensive and relatively ineffective for preparing your case to be won on the merits.

- Lack of broader goal.

- Increases animosity.

- Often leads to a settlement that is a loss for both parties, with no clear winner.

- High risk of losing out on favorable compromises.

- Weakens overall case position more often than strengthening it due to wasted expenses on non-beneficial work, leaving a lower budget for higher-return efforts.

- More likely to lead to a fee-dispute with your client.

- Increases litigation fees and costs for both parties.

TRUE STORY

In a simple case we had, the other side served hundreds of repetitive and irrelevant discovery requests. They were clearly using an Attrition strategy (even though they might not have labeled it such). We threatened to bring a protective order. Eventually, we were able to whittle down their discovery requests and avoid a lot of motion work.

After a few months of similarly unfocused strategies from the other side, they started talking settlement. Because they spent their litigation budget and we avoided engaging, we were able to go into settlement negotiations knowing that we had a war chest remaining while they didn't. At that point, we were able to switch to a more aggressive position, which they could not easily counter since they did not have a budget to do so.

Time Pressure/Deadlines

Description: Deadlines, especially when they seem serious, are extremely powerful. Time Pressure prevents people from properly analyzing the situation, and it makes them react instinctively. If they are unsure, then these reactions will more often than not result in some benefit to you.

If you can add Time Pressure, you can get a tremendous amount of leverage. Almost every lawyer uses deadlines, but they are frequently bluffs. Artificial deadlines, if known to be bluffs, provide no benefit and can often result in a loss to strategic position since later deadlines will lose their power.

You can spot an artificial deadline or bluff if there is no reason supporting it and it is irrationally short. For instance, if trial is six months away and suddenly there is an offer with a ten-day deadline for a response, then you know that it is an artificial deadline and you might get a benefit by ignoring it completely.

Thus, a good counter strategy is to call opposing counsel's bluff on a deadline. If you do, and it turns out they are bluffing, then their subsequent deadlines lose their power. Additionally, if you completely ignore a deadline – not even expressly rejecting it – you will often frustrate opposing counsel.

You should use Time Pressure deliberately. Don't put a deadline on everything, but don't forget to use them either. The ideal use of deadlines is to use them more frequently earlier in a case, and stick to them, to establish that you mean what you say. This will allow you to bluff effectively, and with higher strategic value, later in the case.

SKIPPING THE LEARNING CURVE

When presenting deadlines, give an explanation as to *why* you have chosen the specific date. Otherwise, soften the deadline to maintain credibility (e.g., "we would appreciate a response by Tuesday" instead of "we demand a response by Tuesday.")

Also consider the power of real deadlines (for example, motion and discovery deadlines) and work them into your strategy.

Counter: There are two effective counters: (1) completely ignoring the deadline, or (2) acknowledging it and taking its power away.

Ignoring a deadline will give you the most information and strategic advantage, but carries some risk if your opponent is not bluffing.

If you don't want to completely ignore it, you can acknowledge that your opponent has set a deadline, but at the same time, do not agree to comply with that deadline. Take the approach that you will work diligently but the quality of your work matters and your job cannot be rushed; you will be done when you are done. That means maybe you will respond before their deadline but you might also respond after. You have no way of knowing.

Strategies and Counterstrategies

When countering a Deadline with an acknowledgement, it is important that you are honestly and diligently working on whatever the other side has demanded if that demand is something that you plan to respond to in any manner. For instance, if they demand a counteroffer by a certain date and you don't plan to provide a counteroffer, don't promise to give one. Also, you must keep in mind that statutory deadlines have an effect on whether you can properly utilize this counter: this counter is not intended to be a method of needless delay or to simply buy time. Nor would it allow you to extend deadlines set by statute, rules, or the court. It is intended to send the message that you will not give authority to your opponent's arbitrary rules.

Pros:
- When used effectively, deadlines can put pressure on your opponent, provide structure to your strategy, and give you leverage at key moments.

- Low risk and low effort for you; if your opponent thinks you might be serious, they will perceive a high risk associated with ignoring it.

Cons:
- When used ineffectively or too often, Time Pressure can lose its power and make you look like you're bluffing even when you're not.

- Must be willing to follow through, especially early on to set a precedent.

TRUE STORY

A client came to us in a panic because they received a pre-litigation demand letter setting a strict deadline for payment, and threatening to file suit "the day after the deadline expires" if our client did not accept the settlement amount.

It was our belief, for a variety of reasons, that opposing counsel was bluffing (one major clue was the arbitrariness of the date: there was no statute of limitations issue or other explanation). Our advice was to not respond at all.

Our client was hesitant because this was an employment case in which they had clear liability. Further, in California, the employment laws heavily favor plaintiffs. The threatened damages were in the hundreds of thousands of dollars. But they took our advice.

A month later they received another demand letter with a lower settlement amount, and another "strict deadline." This one we acknowledged with a letter to opposing counsel stating that we would review the situation and get back to them shortly. We responded a few days after their deadline disputing their claims, but not offering money. After a few months of negotiations and no litigation, we reached a settlement for over 90% off the original demand.

If the potential plaintiff's counsel had used an effective Time Pressure strategy, or if we had not implemented a proper counter, our client would have incurred significate legal fees and paid a much higher settlement amount. To make their strategy more effective, opposing counsel should have started the negotiations *without* a strict deadline.

UNCOMMON CASE STRATEGIES

These "uncommon" case strategies require more planning, but can be incredibly effective.

Lay a Trap/Red-herring

Description: A "trap" or red-herring is any series of actions that leads your opponent to go the way you want him to go. This can be extremely difficult since you cannot know how your opponent will react; at most, you can make an educated guess. Too often, people assume they know how the other side will react, pin all their hopes on that assumption, and then get angry when things don't go that way. Worse, they will cling to their planned sequence of events and not adapt to the reality. Nonetheless, when used carefully and with proper contingency planning, a Trap works.

There are several effective results you can get from a Trap. For example: you can Trap someone into lying (and getting caught in that lie), into giving you a particularly useful discovery response, or into focusing on the wrong argument in a brief (as we did in the Decoy example).

One of the most frequent times to use a Trap is during depositions, because you have a lot of control over the process: you have had time to plan out your questions, you have a stack of documents that you selected for the deponent to look at, and you have a good idea, from your preparation, of what the deponent knows and what they want to hide. The deponent, on the other hand, can only guess at what you know.

You can lay Traps in written discovery as well, and can even do it when arguing motions if you plan ahead and deploy information and arguments strategically. But timing is crucial to a Trap. It can be hard to sit on a good piece of evidence, a winning argument, or a gotcha question, but you have to wait until the right moment if you want to use it effectively.

Counter: Avoid falling into Traps by approaching everything with fresh eyes – don't let your opponent frame the issues for you. Prevent your witnesses from falling into Traps by making sure they have a simple story to tell that is consistent with their own memories and the evidence.

Pros:

- Makes the other side do your job for you.

- Looks impressive in the moment.

- Discredits opposing witnesses.

Cons:

- If you do it wrong or too often, it can look like a dirty trick and harm your reputation – remember to be honorable!

- A sophisticated opponent might see through it.

- When it fails, it often fails spectacularly.

Strategies and Counterstrategies

> ## TRUE STORY
>
> We were representing a client in an administrative hearing. At issue was whether there was a "prohibited discharge" flowing off his property and into a lagoon.
>
> On cross-examination at the hearing, I asked a series of questions to get the City's main witness to admit that they had no evidence of actual pollution, but rather, only "natural sediment."
>
> He agreed.
>
> I then got him to admit that the City's only theory is that the "natural sediment" that flows off the property is a prohibited discharge since he just admitted that it was the only thing flowing off the property.
>
> The witness readily admitted that. I then asked "what's naturally at the bottom of the lagoon"?
>
> This eventually led to an award in our favor (it makes no sense to prohibit natural sediment when that is what is at the bottom of the lagoon).

Pick Your Battles

Description: A lot of lawyers will bring a motion or serve discovery simply because they can; or worse, because "that's what they have always done." But just because you can file a motion, doesn't mean you should. A motion to compel, for example, is time consuming, can be risky, and even after a "win" might not get you useful information. Sometimes, it might be better to save the time and money and get the information another way.

Likewise, other motions and filings, such as demurrers, are often a waste of time. If you can't get rid of the whole case and it isn't in your client's best interest to delay things, don't bother with the demurrer: just save your arguments for a motion for summary judgment.

Unless your client has an endless budget and you have endless time, approach motions and discovery carefully and not "just because I can" or "just because this is how it's always done." Especially with contested motions, aim to get value. If you cannot point to a specific benefit of the motion, then it's not valuable.

Counter: Don't mistake this strategy for weakness. When this kind of lawyer takes action, they do it from a position of strength. If you underestimate this strategy, or if have used up all your resources on petty issues, you could easily be outmatched. If your opponent has a reputation for not taking unnecessary action, you have the opportunity to enjoy a pleasant, professional relationship. If you can, take a similar approach and Pick Your Battles, maximizing the chances that your case reaches resolution efficiently, whether through settlement or trial.

Pros:
- Saves time and money.

- Maximizes the chance that what you file is strong. This makes you and your client look good, and promotes a cooperative relationship with opposing counsel, ultimately leading to a better result.

Strategies and Counterstrategies

Cons:

- If you have a very aggressive client or very aggressive opponent, Picking Your Battles might make you look weak in the short term (though it will have long term benefits).

- Risks missing out on strong evidence that you didn't know existed.

TRUE STORY

We faced an opposing counsel who was clearly using an Attrition strategy: their discovery responses were evasive, they were threatening to move for protective orders constantly, and they were making witnesses unavailable for depositions.

Instead of fighting everything, we assembled our evidence and filed a motion for summary judgment.

Turns out, they were not actually ready to fight the case on the merits, and all they could do was yell at me on the phone to try to get me to withdraw the motion.

Since they had already spent an inordinate amount of their client's money on petty and valueless "litigation," the case quickly resolved before their opposition was due.

PLOW AHEAD

Description: From day one, start preparing for trial. Don't overwork; rather, focus on getting prepared. This strategy requires a lot from you mentally.

It requires you to work on your case early, when you probably have other, more urgent, priorities. And it requires you to keep working and preparing even when an extension has granted you a reprieve.

You must resist the urge to procrastinate even in the face of far-away deadlines and the hope of early settlement.

Counter: A lawyer who prepares early and Plows Ahead might be more easily thrown off by last minute changes and short deadlines.

Make sure you are as prepared as your opponent, and don't rely on a fear of moving forward to motivate settlement – focus on the merits of the case, because this lawyer will be very familiar with them.

Pros:
- No matter what happens in your case, you are ready.
- You will always be in the strongest possible negotiating position.
- You will avoid preparing things at the last minute.
- Your work product will be better.

Cons:
- Requires an up-front investment of time and money that may seem to have been "wasted" if your case settles early.
- Can be challenging to communicate the value of this strategy to your client.

Strategies and Counterstrategies

> **TRUE STORY**
>
> We had a mediation scheduled. The day before the mediation, opposing counsel served us with a motion for summary judgment. This is a common tactic to try to apply pressure at the mediation.
>
> But, because we were organized and prepared, we were able to have strong arguments in opposition to discuss at the mediation. We also would have been able to prepare an opposition very quickly.
>
> At the mediation, the other side did not gain leverage despite having filed a motion for summary judgment.

Overwhelm

Description: This strategy is similar to Attrition, but it is different in that it creates the *illusion* that you are overworking the case while not actually creating extra work. This is done by having a high rate of contact with the other side. For instance, most lawyers will put together a large set of interrogatories, requests for admission, and requests for production, and serve it all at once (or maybe space each of those out a little to try to give the other side no respite).

Instead, if each is broken out into multiple sets, and served at frequent intervals, opposing counsel will constantly be scheduling new deadlines and reviewing new documents and their client will constantly have to engage with the case.

Frequent phone calls and emails will also aid in giving the illusion that you are doing more work, and will make the other side feel like you are, when in reality, you have done the same amount but spaced out over a larger period of time.

Counter: Relax and focus on what *you* need to get done. Ask for extensions strategically and keep your information organized to minimize your response time. You could consider "punishing" the strategy by matching it if you have the resources to send a request for every request received. If you don't have the resources (or if their resources make it unlikely that this will Overwhelm them) focus on a larger, more devastating goal, like a motion for summary judgment, while letting them think they have been successful in miring you in their small tasks.

Pros:
- You have control over what your opponent is working on.

- Can make your opponent feel overwhelmed and on their heels.

Cons:
- Can get expensive for both sides if not used skillfully.

- Requires careful planning and organization.

Strategies and Counterstrategies

TRUE STORY

Instead of serving sixty interrogatories in one set, we frequently break it up into multiple sets. Most lawyers will spend similar amounts of time responding to ten interrogatories as they do sixty. Once the first set of responses is received, or shortly before the due date, we serve the next.

The point is to constantly swarm the other side with tasks so that they can't catch their breath, while keeping your requests extremely reasonable. Breaking up your requests also gives you time to think about your case, look at evidence, and review whatever responses they do provide, allowing you to ask for information you might not have known you needed at the start.

Do not confuse this strategy with the common tactic of serving three-hundred interrogatories when sixty would be sufficient. We never serve more discovery than is necessary because useful responses are far more valuable than creating undue burden on opposing counsel. Too many lawyers serve redundant requests for admission and interrogatories. By doing so, they are not focusing their discovery. Worse, they are, in effect, giving opposing counsel permission to cut corners in their responses because of the numerous redundant and irrelevant discovery requests. And then they burden *themselves* with the job of sifting through all those objections and repetitive answers for the few pieces of useful information hidden within it.

Always focus your discovery plan to get the best information!

IN SUMMARY

There are numerous strategies that you can use in approaching a lawsuit. Most lawyers believe they are strategic, but rarely adopt a tailored approach. Instead, they move forward on instinct and habit.

Proper strategy involves knowing your options, their respective strengths and weaknesses, and when to use them.

As critical as it is to have a thorough understanding of the strategies, it is equally as important to have an understanding and ability to switch to another strategy at the right time.

FINAL THOUGHTS
FINDING BALANCE

Final Thoughts

The Tale of the Abusive Deposition

"There once was a legendary lawyer named Rachel. She had been practicing for decades and won every case. Every lawyer in the city knew her name and feared going up against her.

One day, a young, brash lawyer brought a slip-and-fall case against one of Rachel's clients. The young lawyer was determined to make a name for himself by defeating Rachel at trial. The young lawyer took an early deposition of Rachel's client, and used every trick he knew.

After the deposition of Rachel's client, her associate was perplexed. As expected, the transcript reflected the young lawyer's abusive tactics: he asked inappropriate questions, was unprofessional, and even insulted Rachel directly. In fact, as the deposition went on, the young lawyer got more and more aggressive. It was so bad that for the last half of the deposition, there were almost no questions about the case, and the lawyer devolved into almost purely verbal abuse of Rachel and her client.

Yet, not once, in over one-thousand pages of transcript, did Rachel object. Amazingly, the only words Rachel said the whole time were at the beginning when she stated his appearance and at the end when she proposed a stipulation regarding the handling of the transcript.

Horrified, the associate asked Rachel why she hadn't objected, defended herself, or redirected to relevant topics. Rachel explained, 'when someone gives you a gift, why would you reject it?'"

> *""There are not more than five musical notes, yet the combinations of these five give rise to more melodies than can ever be heard.*
>
> *There are not more than five primary colors, yet in combination they produce more hues than can ever be seen.*
>
> *There are not more than five cardinal tastes, yet combinations of them yield more flavors than can ever be tasted."*
>
> *— Sun Tzu*

At the beginning, I asserted that "balance" was the secret to litigation. To apply balance, you need to know which tools are available, as well as how and when to properly use them. If you use the wrong tools or have the wrong timing, your case will be out of balance, and things will go poorly.

If there are a few themes that I hope you took away from this book they are:

- learn to enjoy the law,
- dedicate yourself to improving, and
- never accept that "the way things have always been done" is necessarily the best way to do something (it might be, but you should always question it).

While this book is organized in a manner that builds on the chapters beforehand, you should reference the different parts as applicable.

For instance, you may want to start a case by trying to explore the different parts that make up "the math." Or maybe you may discern an opponent's "deep dark secret" early on and then review the strategies to figure out the best one to leverage. At other times, you may find yourself feeling frustrated and need an "attitude adjustment" to get back on track.

While this book has given you the tools to excel at litigation, you cannot become proficient without putting them together and using them. But how do *you* learn which tools work best for *you*?

To that end, the next step you should take is to create a document titled "lessons learned." As you reflect on the outcomes of motions, depositions, trials, negotiations, etc., keep notes in this document about how you can improve in the future.

Most of this book is an extension of my own "lessons learned" file.

Some additional examples, that did not make it into this book, are:

- "For oral argument: plan phrases and concepts ahead of time. Be careful ad-libbing. Don't tell judge what he's thinking or what he likes to do."

- "Categorize arguments/points/facts as major or minor. Then get rid of as many minor points as possible because they tend to distract. Try to get the points down to three or four. This applies to trials and briefs."

- "On cross: Ditch questions that might possibly come off petty."

You should update your "lessons learned" file frequently, and review it on occasion.

Similarly, in the same file (or a separate one if you prefer) keep a "strategy index." Here, you will keep track of the strategies you use and their outcome. For instance, did you try a "Play Dumb" strategy against a DIY lawyer? Did it work? Can you evaluate why it was or was not effective? Would another strategy possibly have been more effective?

After some time, you will notice that certain strategies work better in certain circumstances. Use your strategy index to guide your decision making in the future. I cannot give you a complete strategy index because strategies that work for me in certain circumstances might not work for you in the same situation – everyone's execution will necessarily be slightly different.

Lastly, buy and read some of the books on the further reading list. Don't try to pick the ones that you think would be the most "useful," rather start by reading the ones you think would be the most interesting.

You should also feel free to subscribe to my YouTube channel where I discuss legal ethics and best practices.

Final Thoughts

Don't worry if you feel like you can't implement all of the lessons detailed in this book. This book does not summarize the minimum level of ability needed to be competent or to satisfy an adequate standard of practice to avoid a malpractice claim. Those requirements are far lower than the skills taught in this book. Indeed, sometimes you may have no choice but to break from the suggestions in this book.

This book is intended to elevate your skills; to help you go from competent to exceptional. The lessons will have different amounts of relevance to you depending on your practice area, environment, and experience. As such, this book can be used as a reference book, or even just as a motivational source whenever you feel overwhelmed.

In the end, however you are able to use the book, I hope that you find it valuable in your career!

FURTHER READING

In an attempt to continuously improve various skills, I have read dozens of books on different subjects. I encourage you to do the same!

Here, I present a curated list for you to get started.

Some of these might have updated their editions since I purchased my copy. I will mark the edition that I have if indicated in the copy I own.

This is not a complete list; rather, it's a small list from books that I have read. If you come across a book that's not on this list and want to know if I have read it or if I have an opinion about it, feel free to email me.

Duarte, Nancy. *Slide:ology*. O'Reilly Media, 2008.

This is an excellent book about presentations. If you might ever give a lecture or speech, then you should read this book. Although it is not specifically designed for lawyers, every trial attorney should own a copy because a closing argument is little more than a presentation. The concepts and techniques in this book will at least double your effectiveness at trial.

Forsyth, Mark. *The Elements of Eloquence*. Berkley Books, 2014.

This book is a great handbook on rhetorical devices (compositional techniques or turns of phrases). You do not need to memorize the devices, such as "antithesis," "adynaton," or "anaphora" (the list itself being an example of "alliteration"); rather, reading through this book will make you aware of dozens of these devices. If you can effectively incorporate rhetorical devices into your writing and speech, you will sound more witty and be more persuasive.

Gardner, James A. *Legal Argument: The Structure and Language of Effective Advocacy.* **2nd ed. LexisNexis, 2007.**

In Part II, I explained that "logic" is a necessary skill and gave a very brief overview of structuring legal argument. *Legal Argument* by James A. Gardner is a detailed explanation of logical reasoning tailored towards law. It is interesting, straightforward, and truly necessary for any lawyer to own.

Garner, Bryan A. *The Winning Brief.* **3rd ed. Oxford University Press, 2014.**

Bryan Garner is probably the most prolific writer on legal writing that has ever lived. I own a few of his books, but if I had to point to a single one that is a must-own, it would be *The Winning Brief.* While it is tailored towards appellate lawyers, it is no less applicable to trial-level litigators.

Garrity, Jim. *10,000 Depositions Later.* **2nd Ed. Ross & Rubin, 2016.**

If you might ever have to take or defend a deposition, you should read this book. It has concrete and straightforward tips that are applicable in real-world situations. Amazon shows that there has since been a Third Edition that has a significant update on the version I have read.

Guberman, Ross. *Point Made.* **2nd ed. Oxford University Press, 2014.**

You can never have too many writing books! This is another that is specifically tailored towards lawyers. It has many (maybe hundreds) of short examples to better explain the concepts.

Johnson, Brian K., and Hunter, Marsha. *The Articulate Advocate.* **2nd ed. Crown King Books, 2016.**

I have not found many books on how to conduct your body while presenting. This is an amazing book on exactly that and is tailored towards lawyers. Most lawyers would immediately benefit if they even only read the first few chapters about how to stand and how to gesture properly!

Read, Shane. *Turning Points at Trial.* **Westway Publishing, 2017.**

I own three books by Shane Read (*Turning Points at Trial*, *Winning at Deposition*, and *Winning at Trial*). *Turning Points at Trial* covers more than just the "trial." It also includes depositions and appellate advocacy. And he does it from the points of view of some of the Nation's best attorneys.

Rosen, David. *99 Negotiating Strategies.* **Ross & Rubin, 2016.**

This is an extremely short, but valuable, book. Although it is not tailored towards lawyers, it is still applicable to them. Most of the 99 strategies only have a couple of paragraphs of explanation. So it provides a good foundation into negotiation, but not an in-depth education.

Spence, Gerry. *Win Your Case.* **St. Martin's Griffin, 2005.**

Gerry Spence may be one of the best lawyers that has ever lived, and is also a prolific author. *Win Your Case* is not really a "how-to" book. Although it contains technique, it is more of an explanation of his philosophy on law and life. If you think that a book on raw technique is more valuable than a "softer" book, then you probably need the lessons learned in *Win Your Case*.

Trachtman, Joel P. *The Tools of Argument.* **CreateSpace Independent Publishing Platform, 2013.**

Persuasion is very difficult to teach. But lawyers cannot be persuasive without knowing how to build effective argument. And there is a difference between "argument" and "arguing." This book summarizes, and provides "point – counterpoint" examples, into various types of legal arguments.

Voss, Chris, and Raz, Tahl. *Never Split the Difference.* **Random House Business Books, 2016.**

This is another book that is not specifically tailored to lawyers, but is invaluable for them. The author is a former FBI hostage negotiator. The negotiation tools are demonstrated through real-life examples, making this not just an educational book, but also extremely entertaining.

ABOUT AARON SHECHET

Aaron Shechet is admitted to practice law in California, Washington State, and Washington D.C. He has represented businesses and high net-worth families in complex litigation and as general counsel.

In addition, Aaron has dedicated his legal career to exploring legal ethics and best practices. Aaron has frequently spoken, written, and been interviewed on these subjects, as well as advising other lawyers. He was an expert witness regarding legal fees in Phil Spector's lawsuit against Robert Shapiro.

Aaron maintains a YouTube channel discussing legal ethics and best practices, which can be found at:

https://www.youtube.com/c/AaronShechet

www.ingramcontent.com/pod-product-compliance
Lightning Source LLC
LaVergne TN
LVHW011419080426
835512LV00005B/147